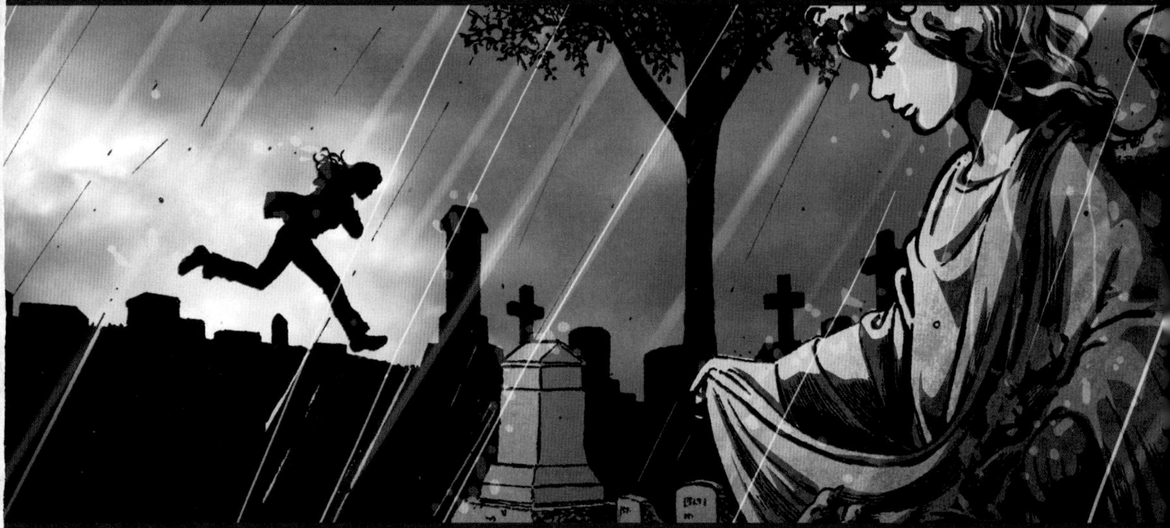

Cemetery Girl

BOOK ONE: THE PRETENDERS

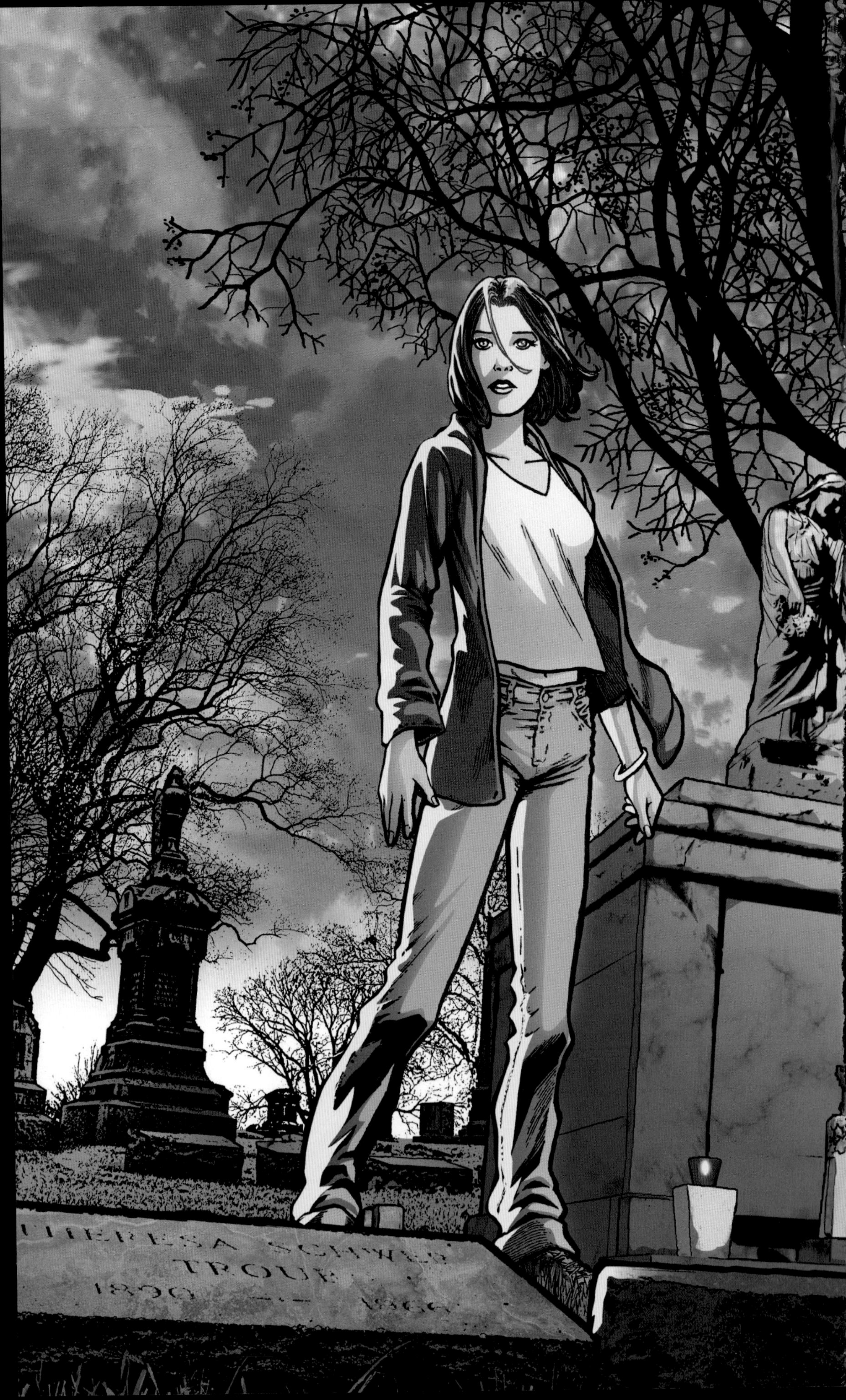

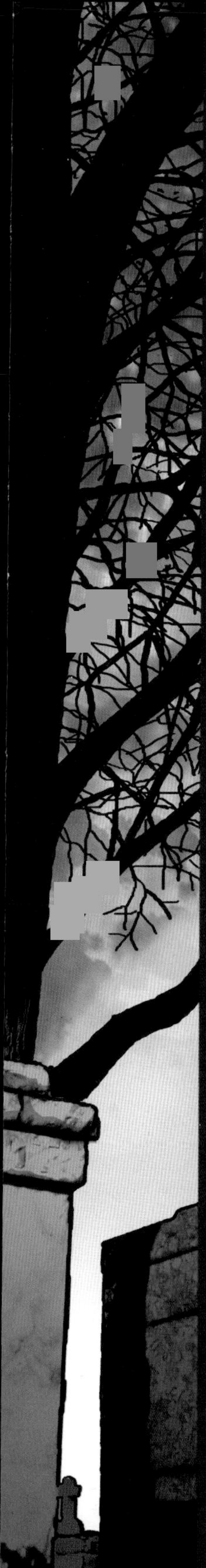

CHARLAINE HARRIS
CHRISTOPHER GOLDEN

CEMETERY GIRL

BOOK ONE: THE PRETENDERS

ART BY **DON KRAMER**

COLORS BY **DANIELE RUDONI**

LETTERS BY **JACOB BASCLE**

First published in the USA 2014 by the Penguin Group
First published in Great Britain in 2014 by

Jo Fletcher Books
An imprint of Quercus
55 Baker Street
7th Floor, South Block
London
W1U 8EW

A CIP catalogue record for this book is available
from the British Library

ISBN 978 0 85738 908 4 (HB)
ISBN 978 1 78087 520 0 (TPB)
ISBN 978 1 78087 370 1 (EBOOK)

10 9 8 7 6 5 4 3 2 1

Illustrations including cover by Don Kramer
Colors including cover by Daniele Rudoni

Printed and bound in Portugal

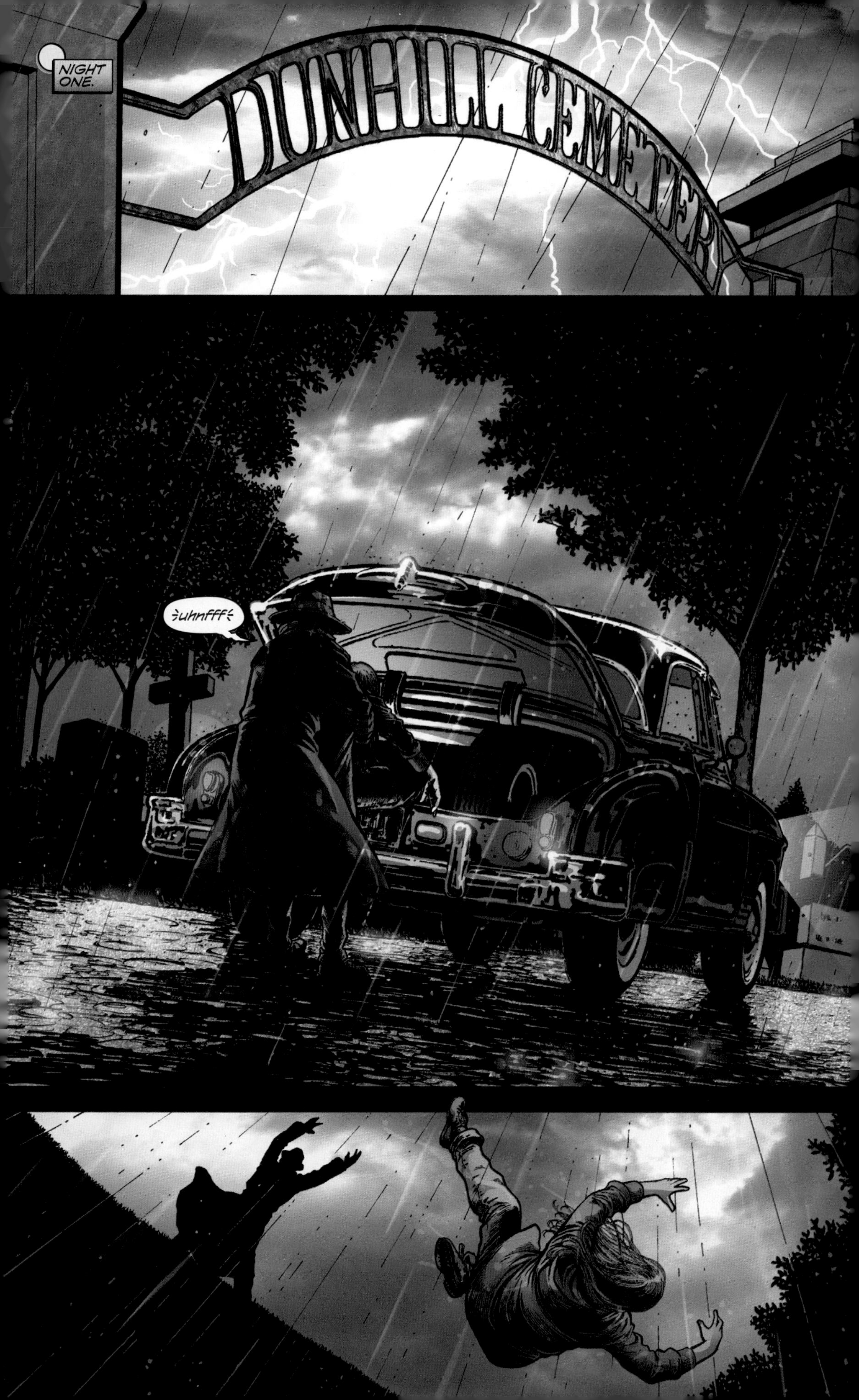
NIGHT ONE.
DUNHILL CEMETERY
uhnfff

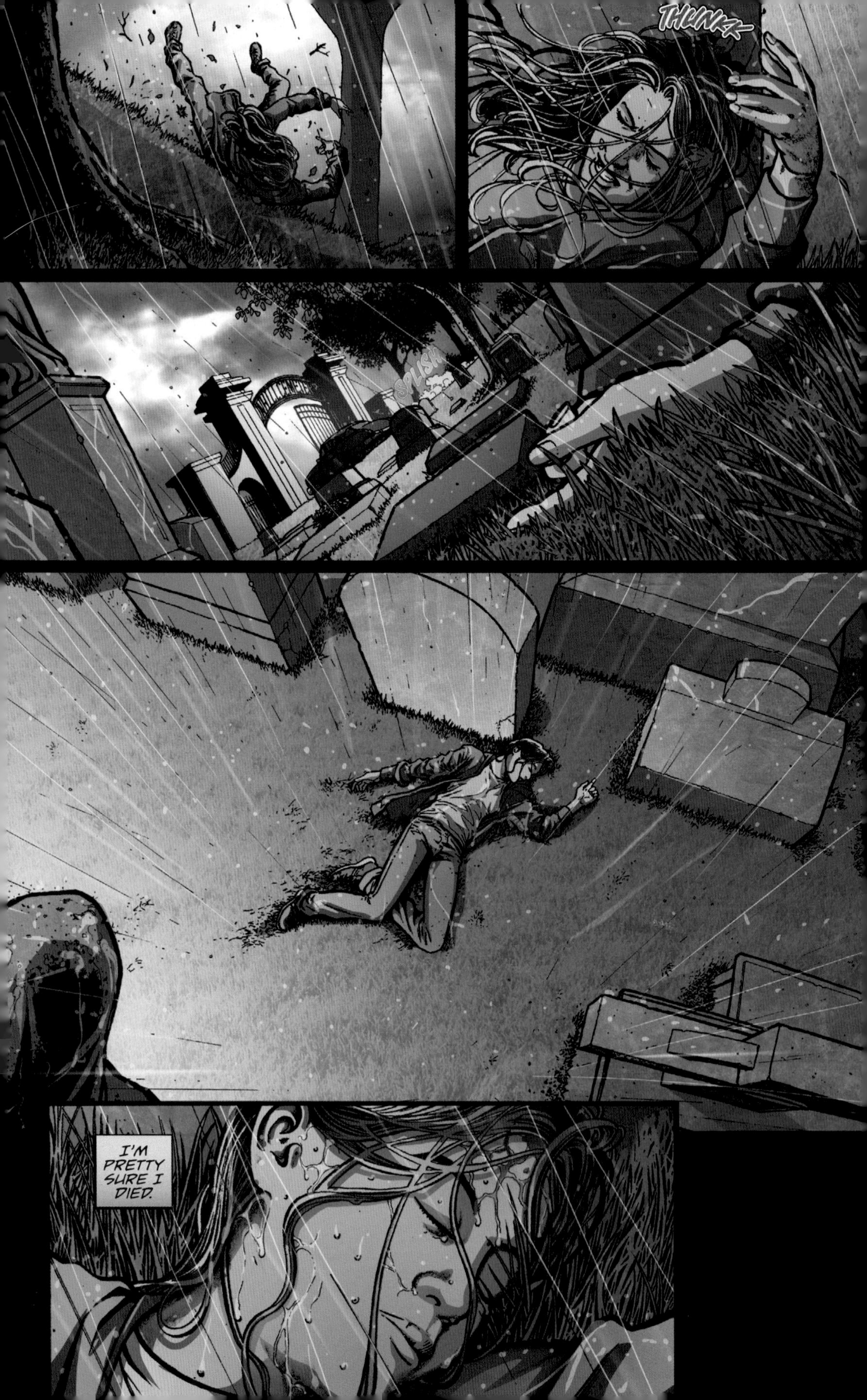
THUNK
SPLISH
I'M PRETTY SURE I DIED.

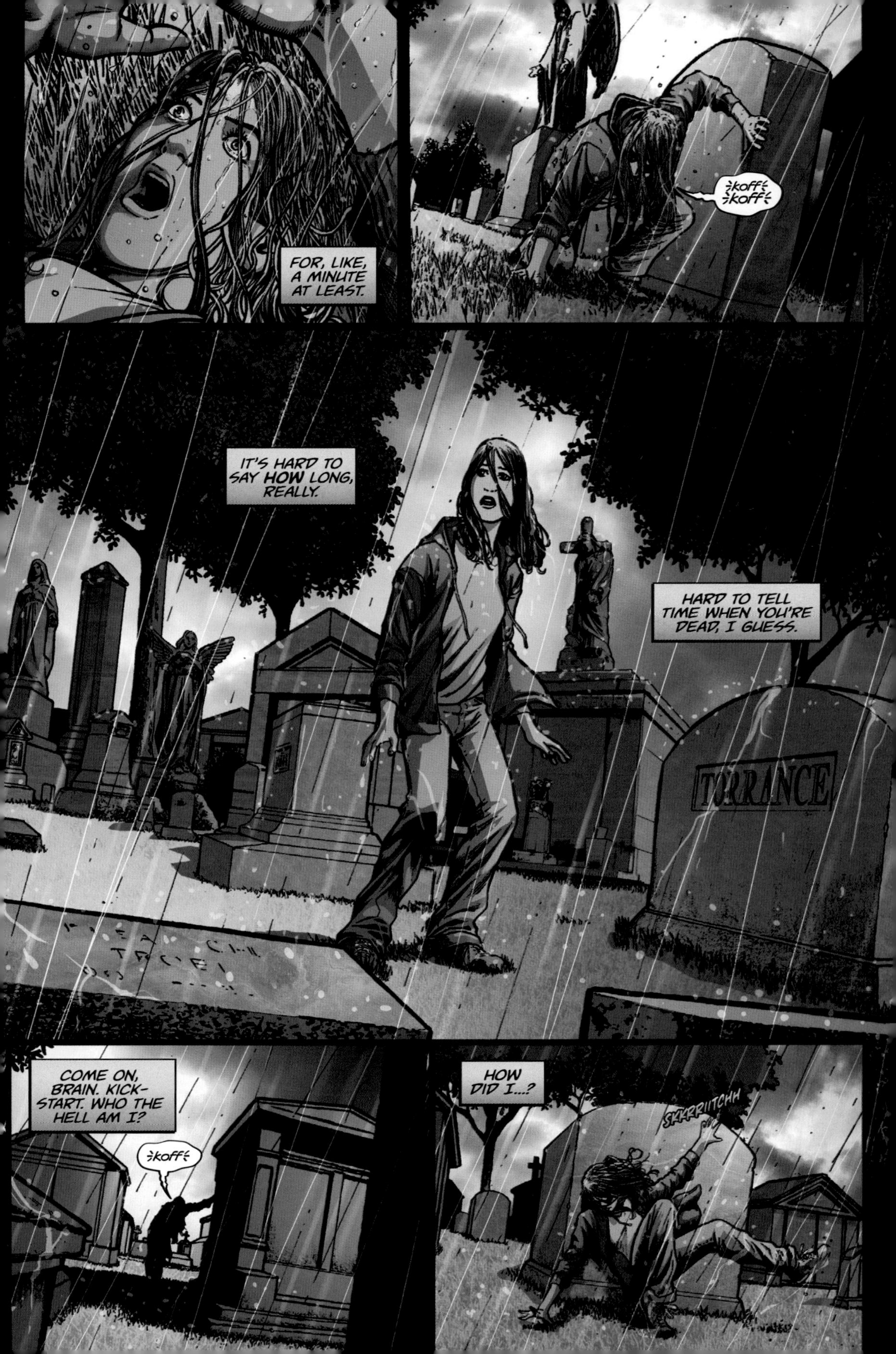
FOR, LIKE, A MINUTE AT LEAST.
koff koff
IT'S HARD TO SAY HOW LONG, REALLY.
HARD TO TELL TIME WHEN YOU'RE DEAD, I GUESS.
TORRANCE
COME ON, BRAIN. KICK-START. WHO THE HELL AM I?
koff
HOW DID I...?
SKKRRIITCHH

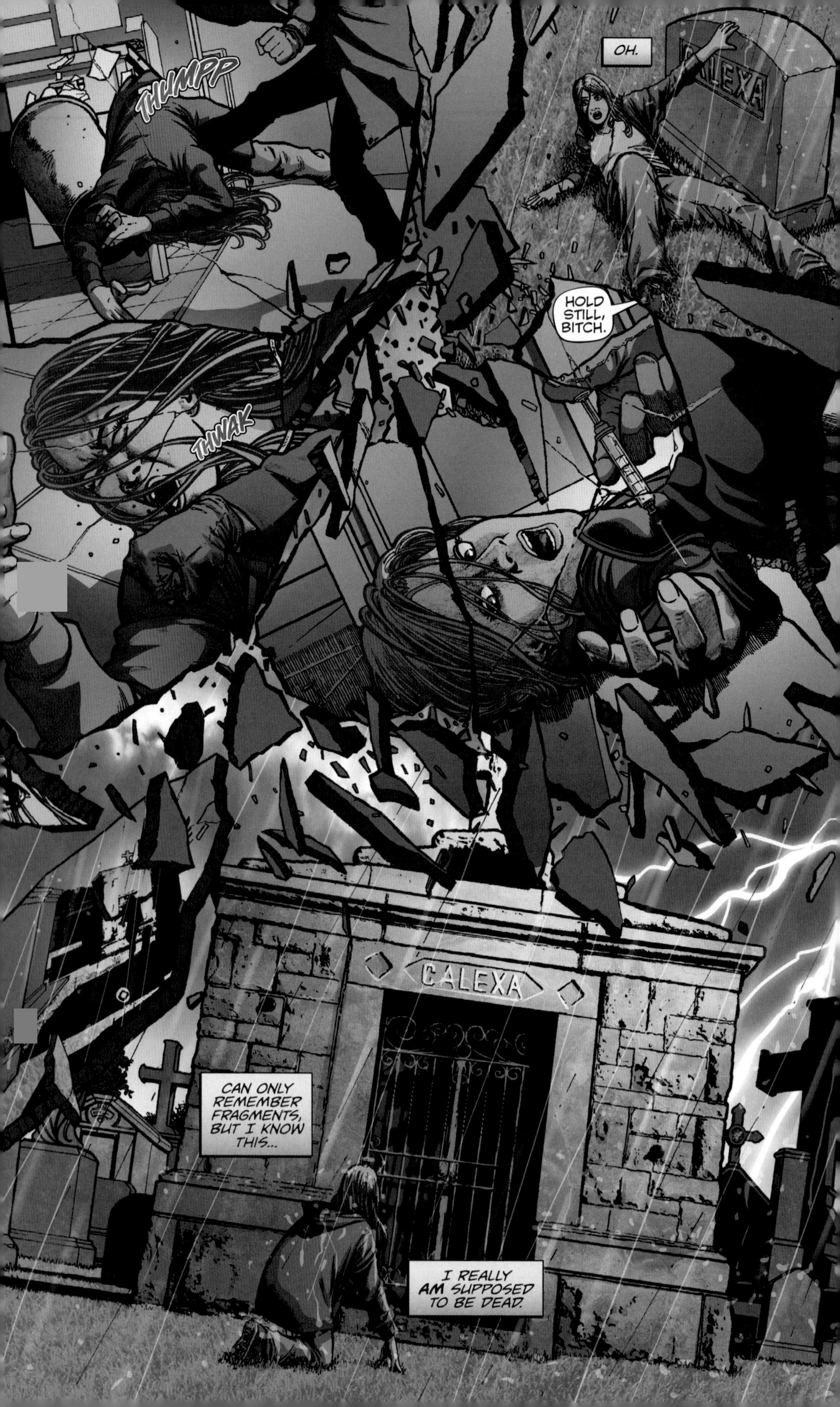
THUMPP
OH.
HOLD STILL, BITCH.
THWAK
CALEXA
CAN ONLY REMEMBER FRAGMENTS, BUT I KNOW THIS...
I REALLY AM SUPPOSED TO BE DEAD.

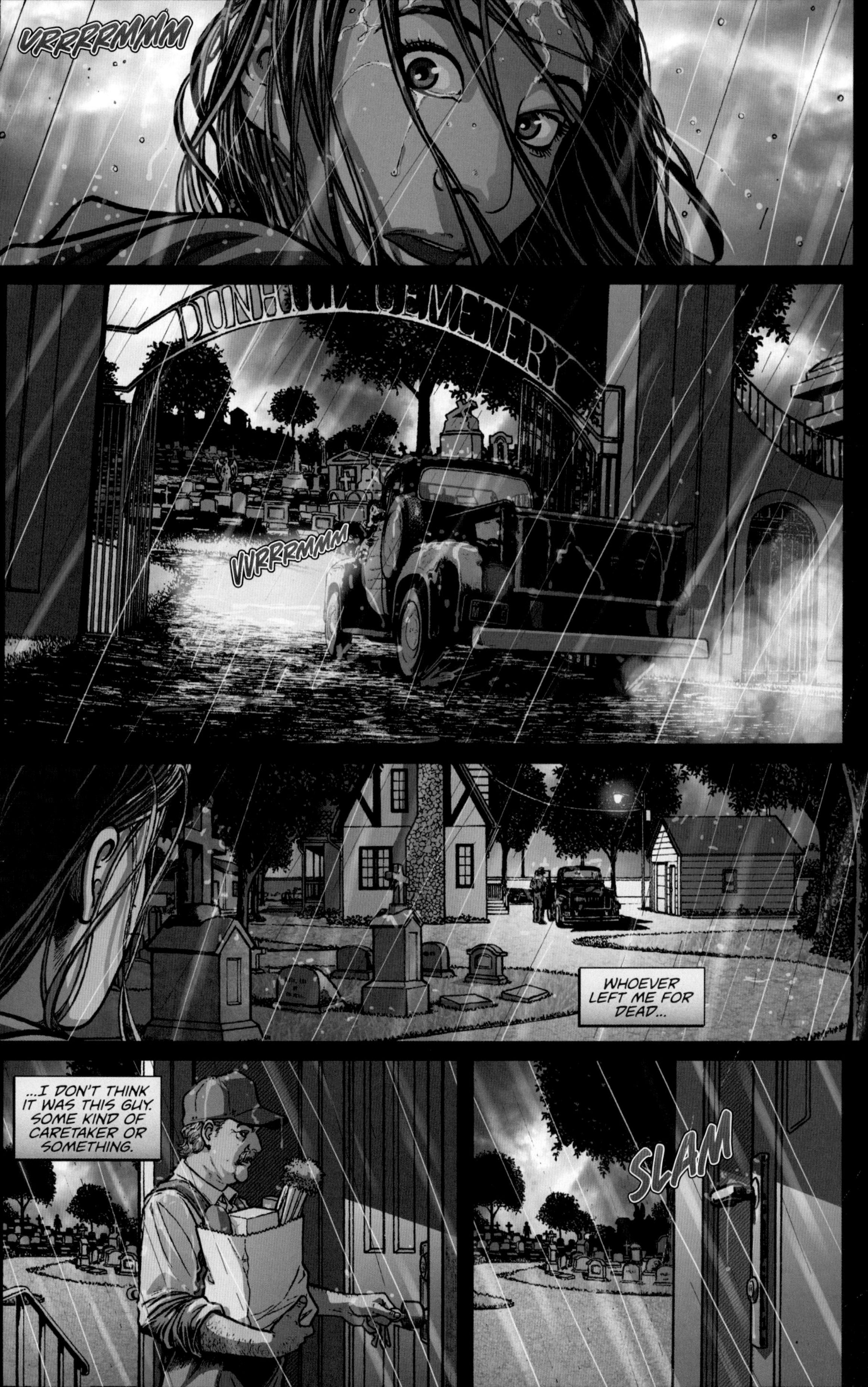
VRRRRMMMM
VVRRRMMM
WHOEVER LEFT ME FOR DEAD...
...I DON'T THINK IT WAS THIS GUY. SOME KIND OF CARETAKER OR SOMETHING.
SLAM

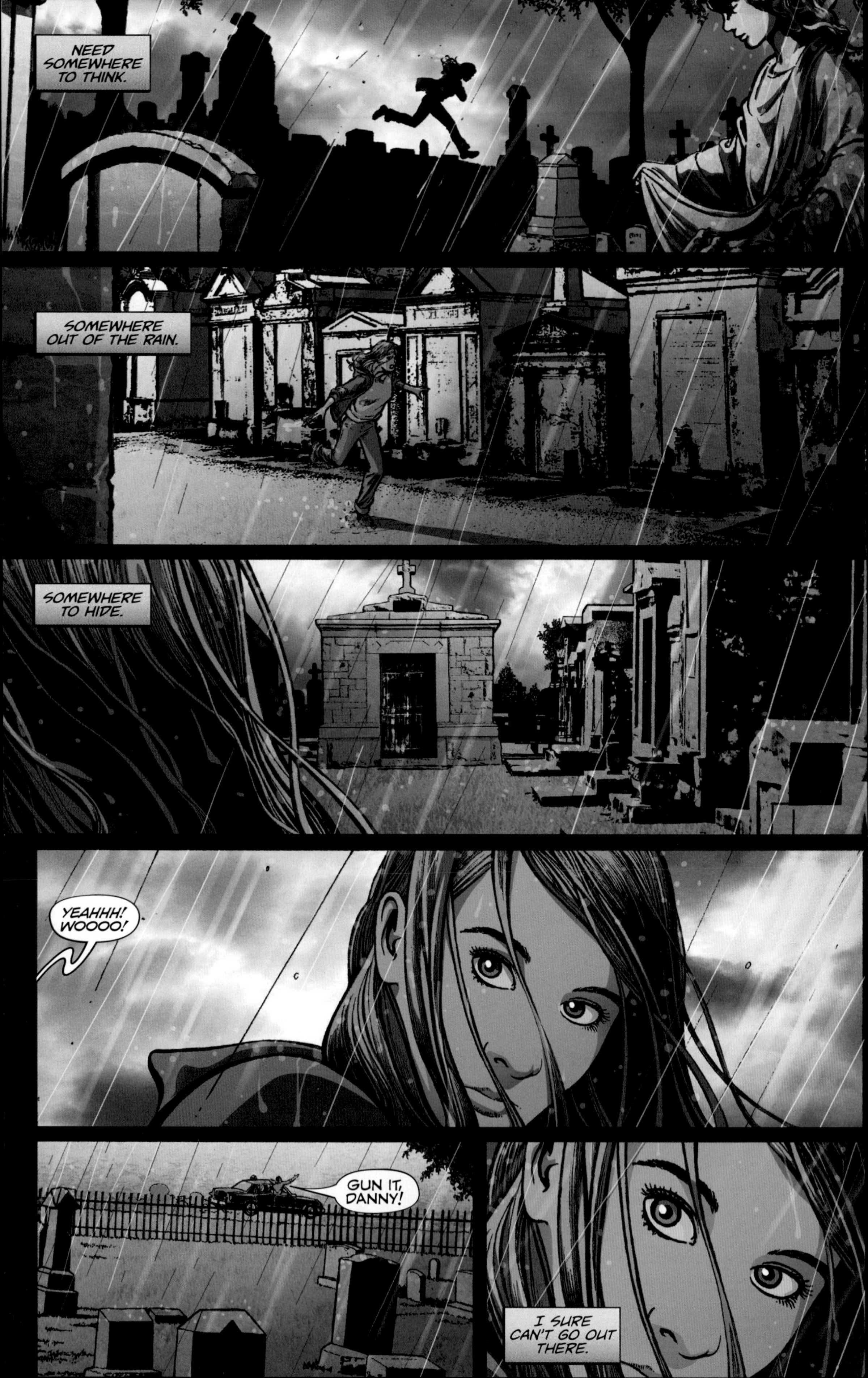
NEED SOMEWHERE TO THINK.
SOMEWHERE OUT OF THE RAIN.
SOMEWHERE TO HIDE.
YEAHHH! WOOOO!
GUN IT, DANNY!
I SURE CAN'T GO OUT THERE.

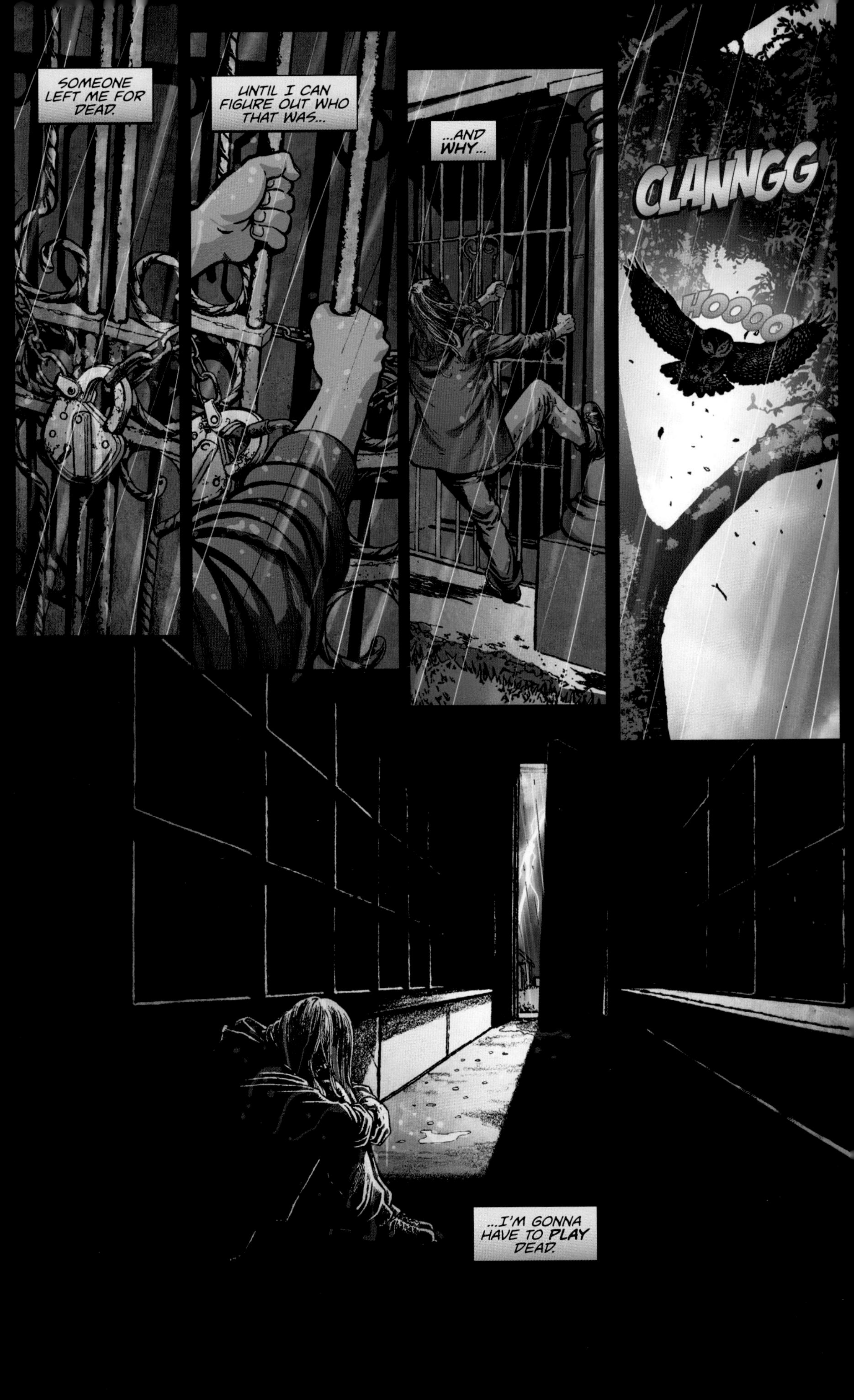
SOMEONE LEFT ME FOR DEAD.
UNTIL I CAN FIGURE OUT WHO THAT WAS...
...AND WHY...
CLANNGG
HOOOO
...I'M GONNA HAVE TO PLAY DEAD.

WHIRRRRR

WHERE...?

CEMETERY. RIGHT.

GREAT.

WHIRRRRR

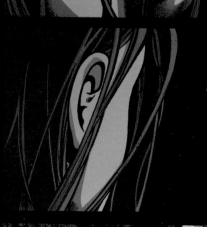

...I'M SAYIN' I DIDN'T TRAMPLE THE DAMN FLOWERS.

I AIN'T EVEN BEEN OVER THAT SIDE OF THE PLACE THIS MORNIN'.

IT'S THE DAMN KIDS, MAN.

I HAVE TO LEAVE. IF HE NOTICES THE GATE'S BEEN FORCED, HE'LL FIND ME.

WHIRRRRR

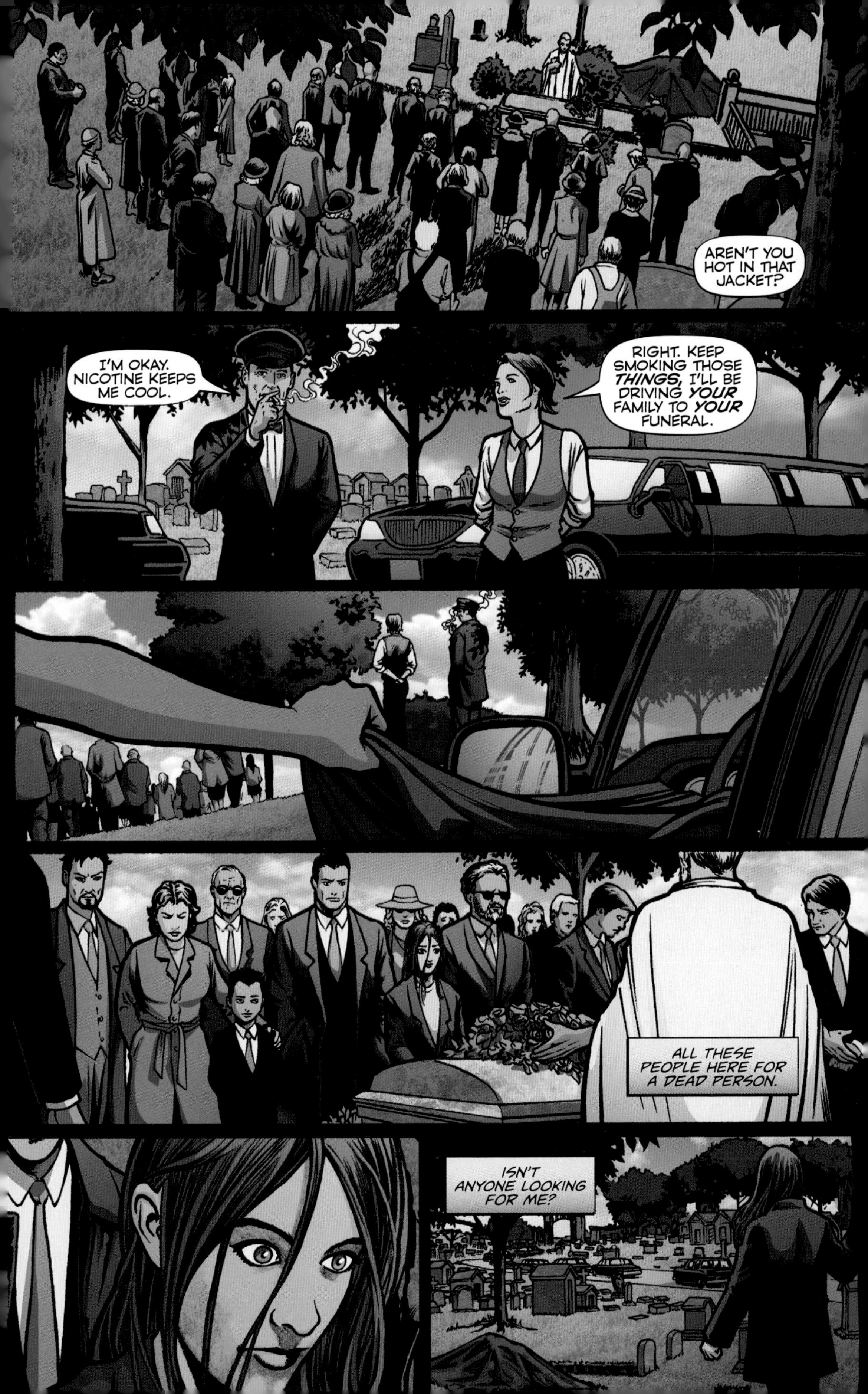
AREN'T YOU HOT IN THAT JACKET?
I'M OKAY. NICOTINE KEEPS ME COOL.
RIGHT. KEEP SMOKING THOSE *THINGS,* I'LL BE DRIVING *YOUR* FAMILY TO *YOUR* FUNERAL.
ALL THESE PEOPLE HERE FOR A DEAD PERSON.
ISN'T ANYONE LOOKING FOR ME?

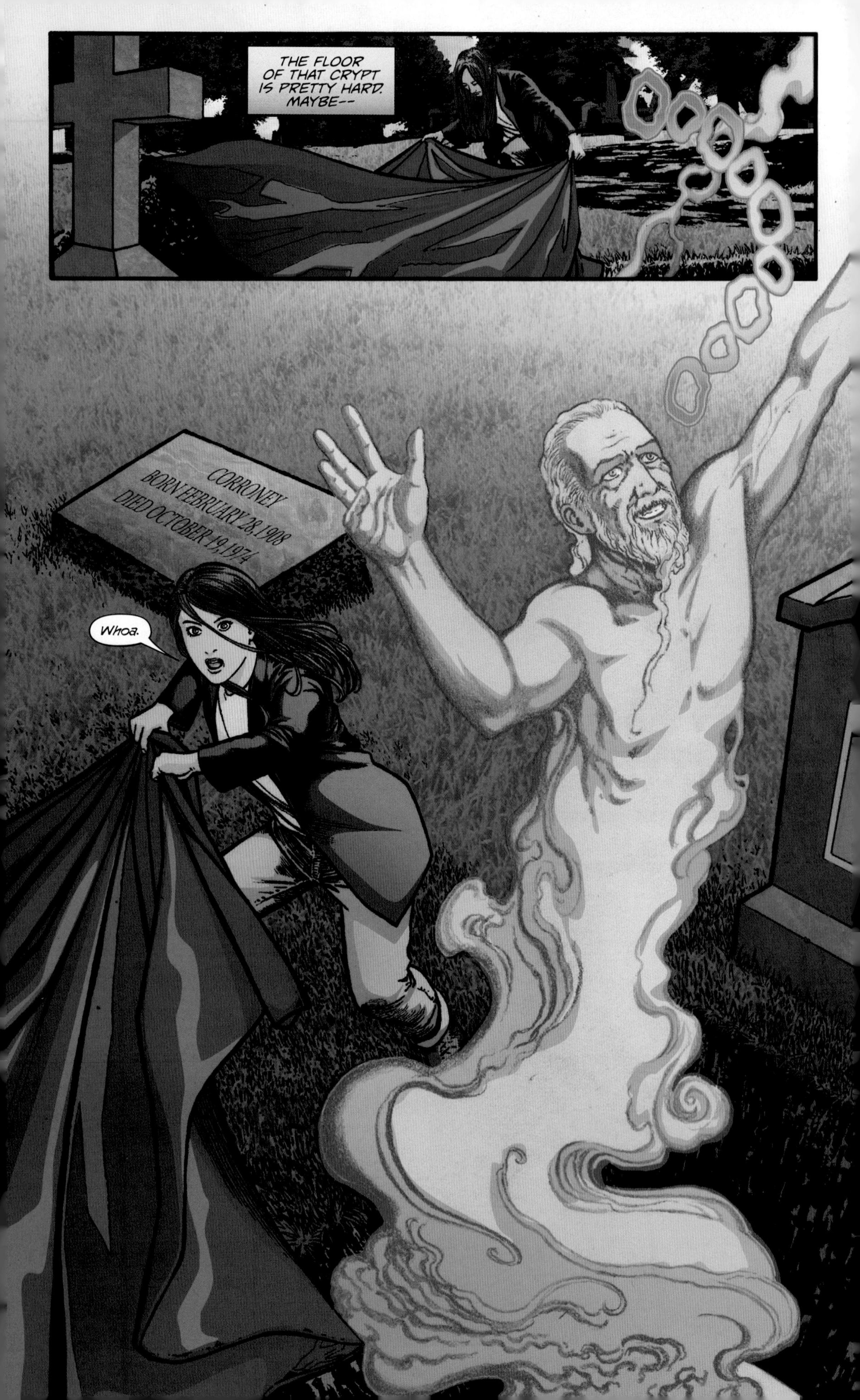
THE FLOOR OF THAT CRYPT IS PRETTY HARD. MAYBE--
CORRONEY
BORN FEBRUARY 28, 1908
DIED OCTOBER 19, 1974
Whoa.

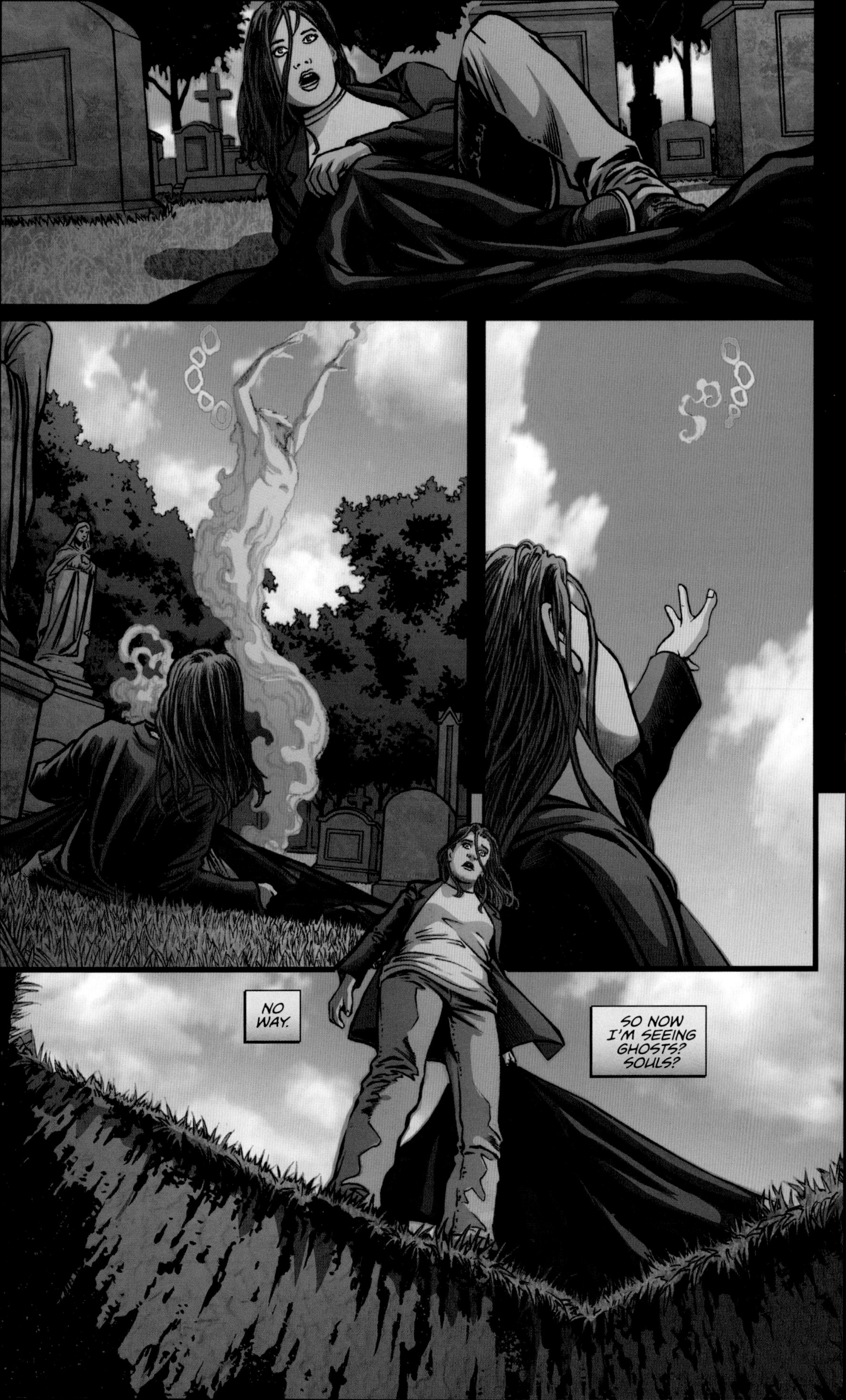
NO WAY.
SO NOW I'M SEEING GHOSTS? SOULS?

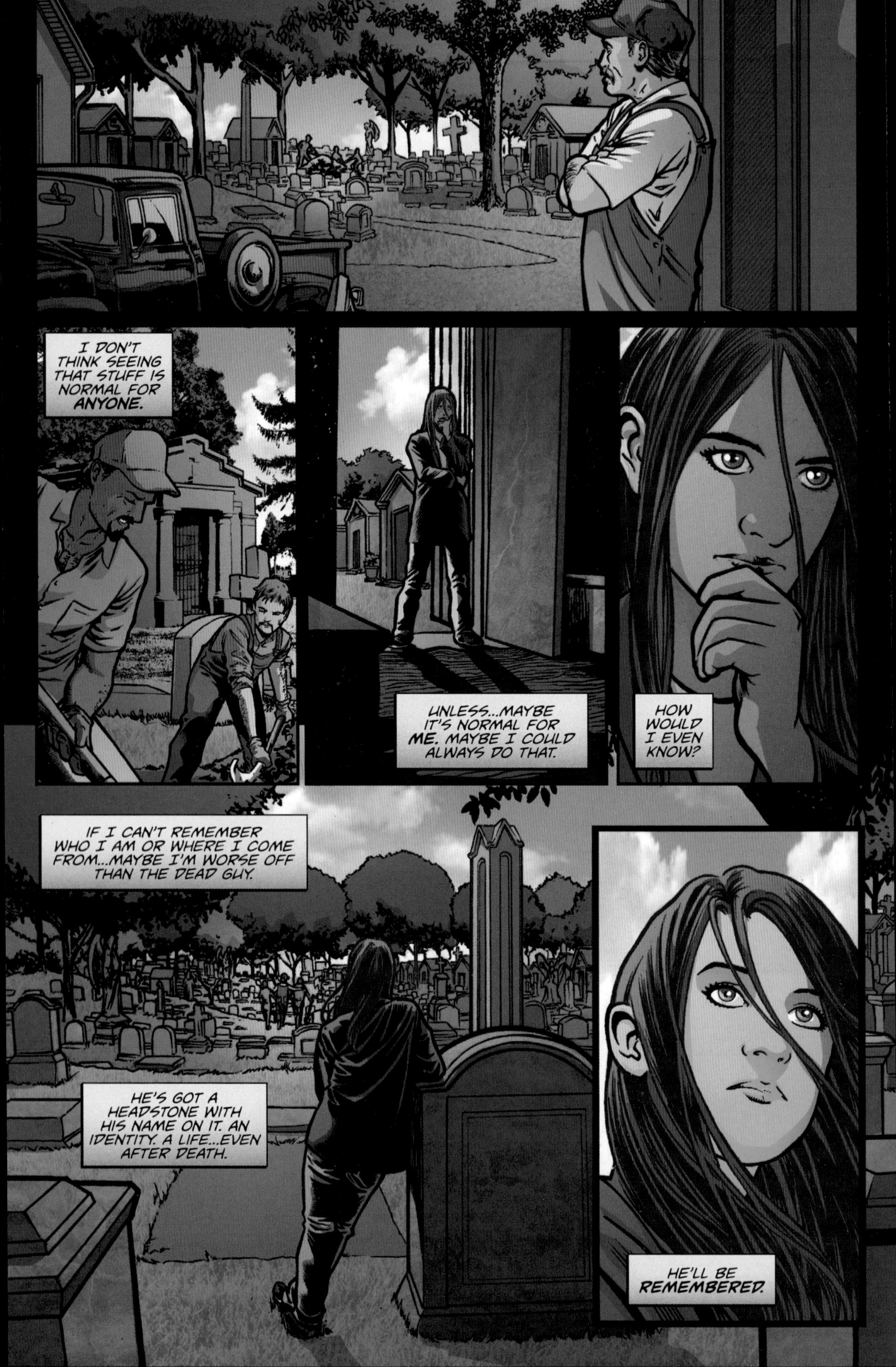
I DON'T THINK SEEING THAT STUFF IS NORMAL FOR ANYONE.
UNLESS...MAYBE IT'S NORMAL FOR ME. MAYBE I COULD ALWAYS DO THAT.
HOW WOULD I EVEN KNOW?
IF I CAN'T REMEMBER WHO I AM OR WHERE I COME FROM...MAYBE I'M WORSE OFF THAN THE DEAD GUY.
HE'S GOT A HEADSTONE WITH HIS NAME ON IT. AN IDENTITY. A LIFE...EVEN AFTER DEATH.
HE'LL BE REMEMBERED.

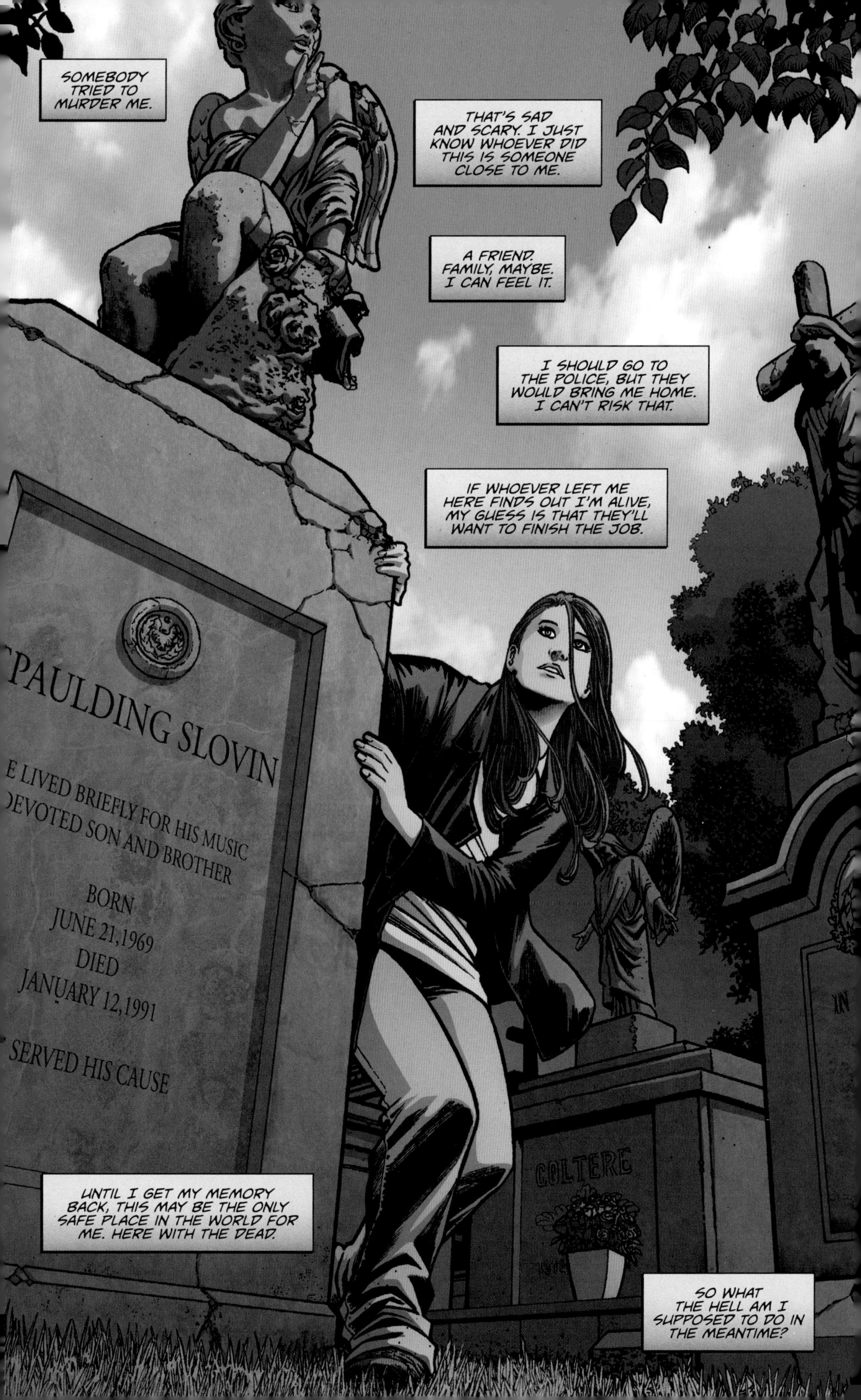

SOMEBODY TRIED TO MURDER ME.
THAT'S SAD AND SCARY. I JUST KNOW WHOEVER DID THIS IS SOMEONE CLOSE TO ME.
A FRIEND. FAMILY, MAYBE. I CAN FEEL IT.
I SHOULD GO TO THE POLICE, BUT THEY WOULD BRING ME HOME. I CAN'T RISK THAT.
IF WHOEVER LEFT ME HERE FINDS OUT I'M ALIVE, MY GUESS IS THAT THEY'LL WANT TO FINISH THE JOB.
BORN
JUNE 21,1969
DIED
JANUARY 12,1991
SERVED HIS CAUSE
COLTERE
UNTIL I GET MY MEMORY BACK, THIS MAY BE THE ONLY SAFE PLACE IN THE WORLD FOR ME. HERE WITH THE DEAD.
SO WHAT THE HELL AM I SUPPOSED TO DO IN THE MEANTIME?

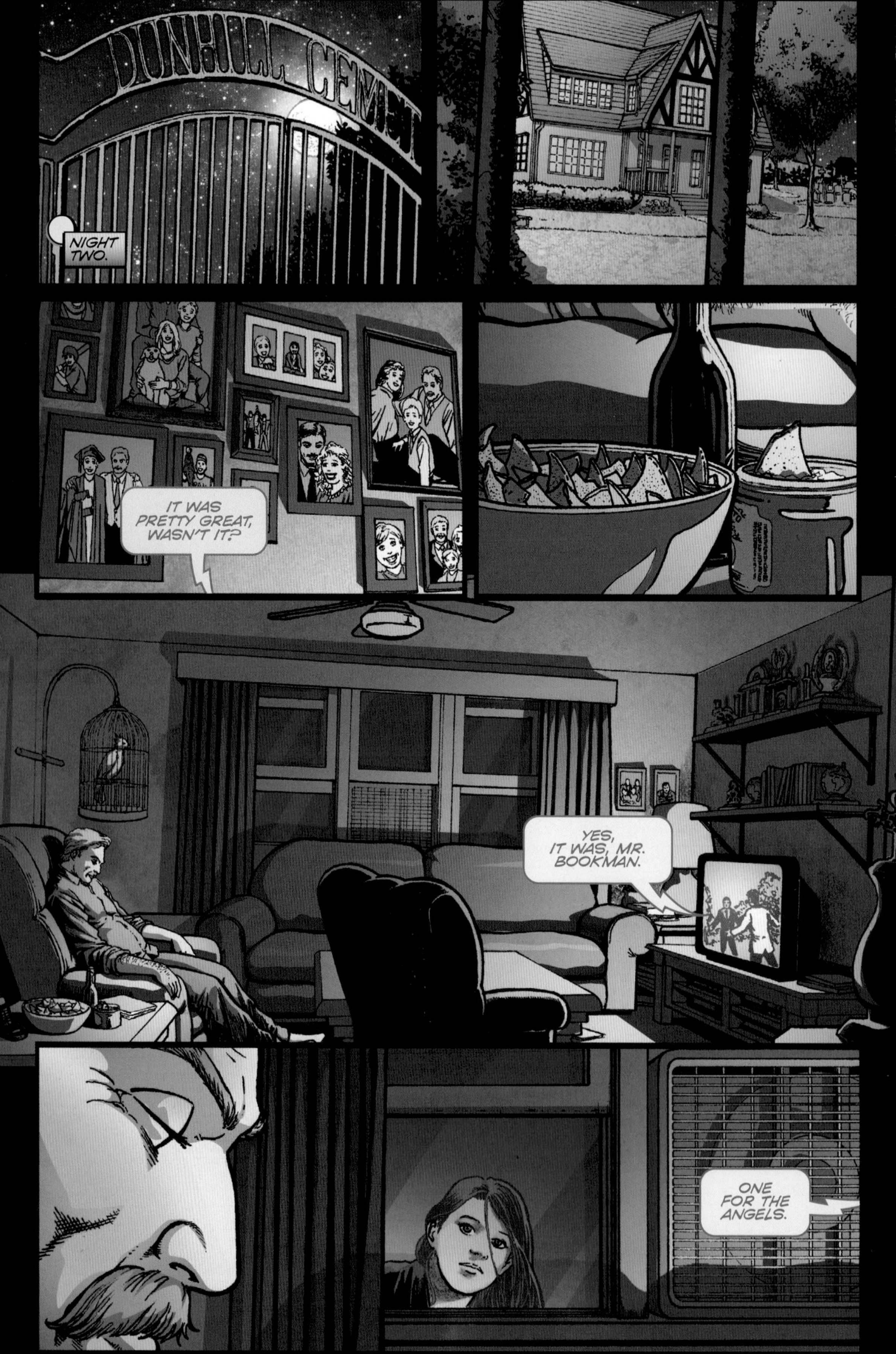
NIGHT TWO.
IT WAS PRETTY GREAT, WASN'T IT?
YES, IT WAS, MR. BOOKMAN.
ONE FOR THE ANGELS.

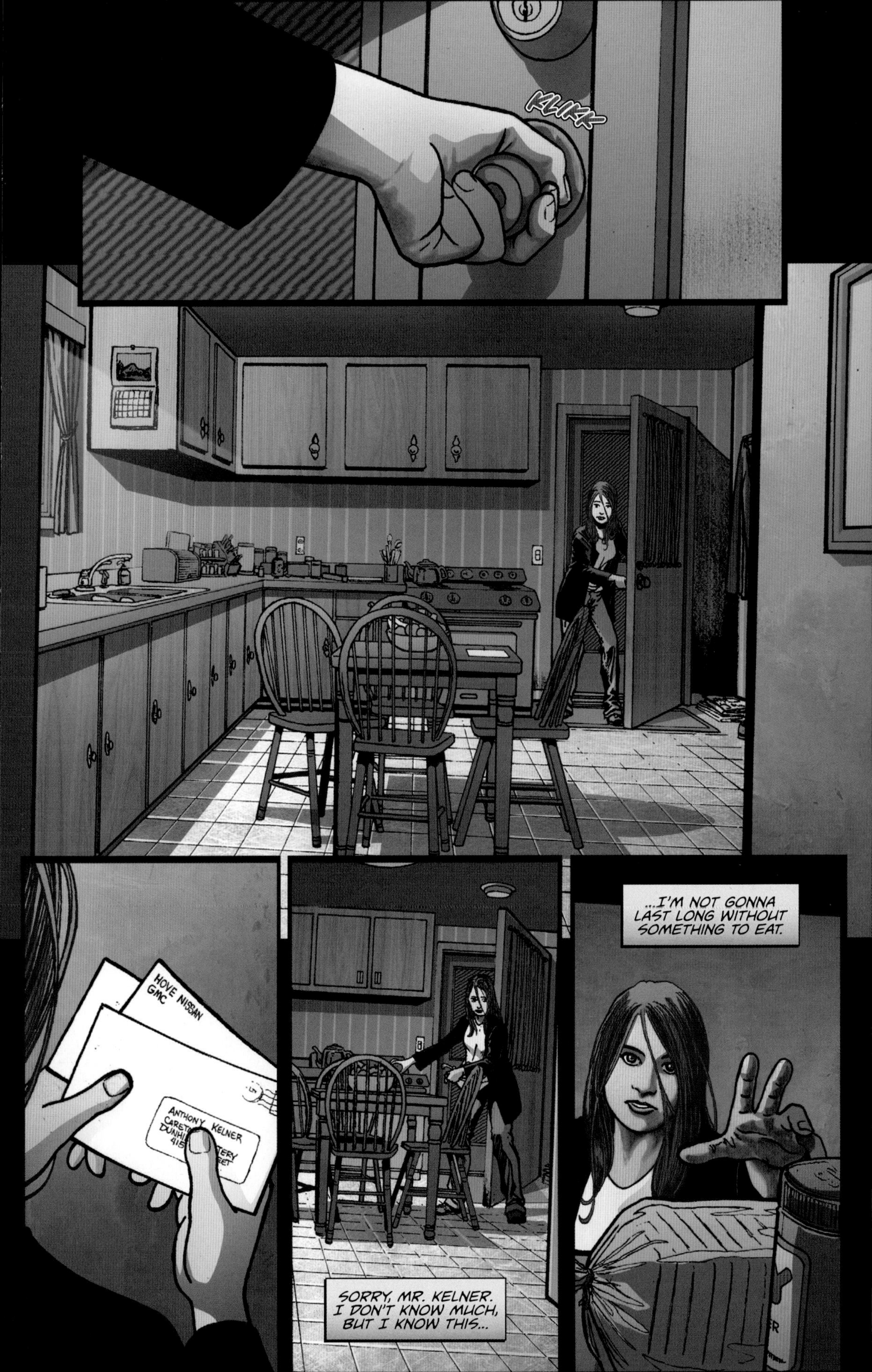
KLIKK
HOVE NISSAN
GMC
ANTHONY KELNER
SORRY, MR. KELNER. I DON'T KNOW MUCH, BUT I KNOW THIS...
...I'M NOT GONNA LAST LONG WITHOUT SOMETHING TO EAT.

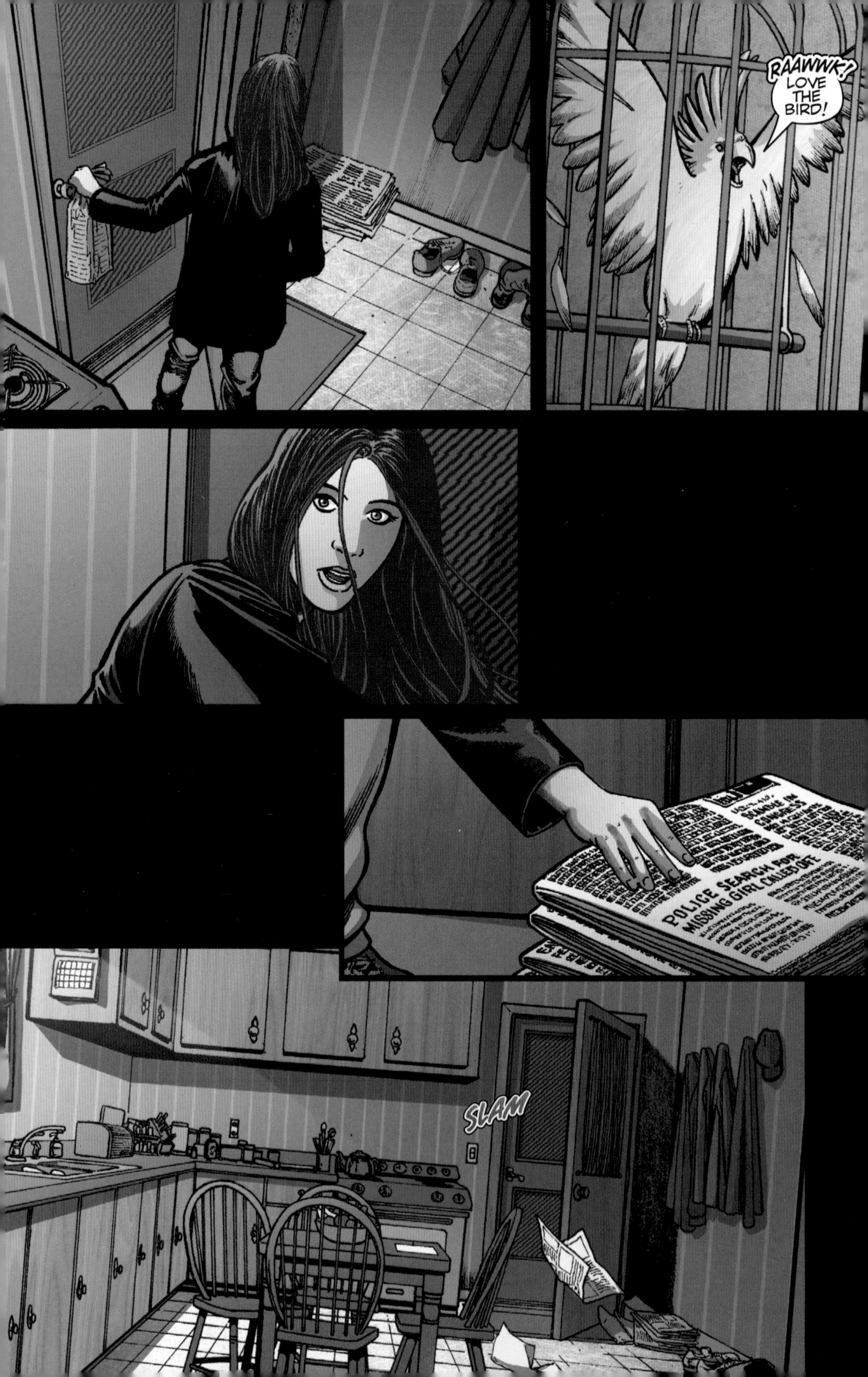
RAAWWK! LOVE THE BIRD!
POLICE SEARCH FOR MISSING GIRL CALLED OFF
SLAM

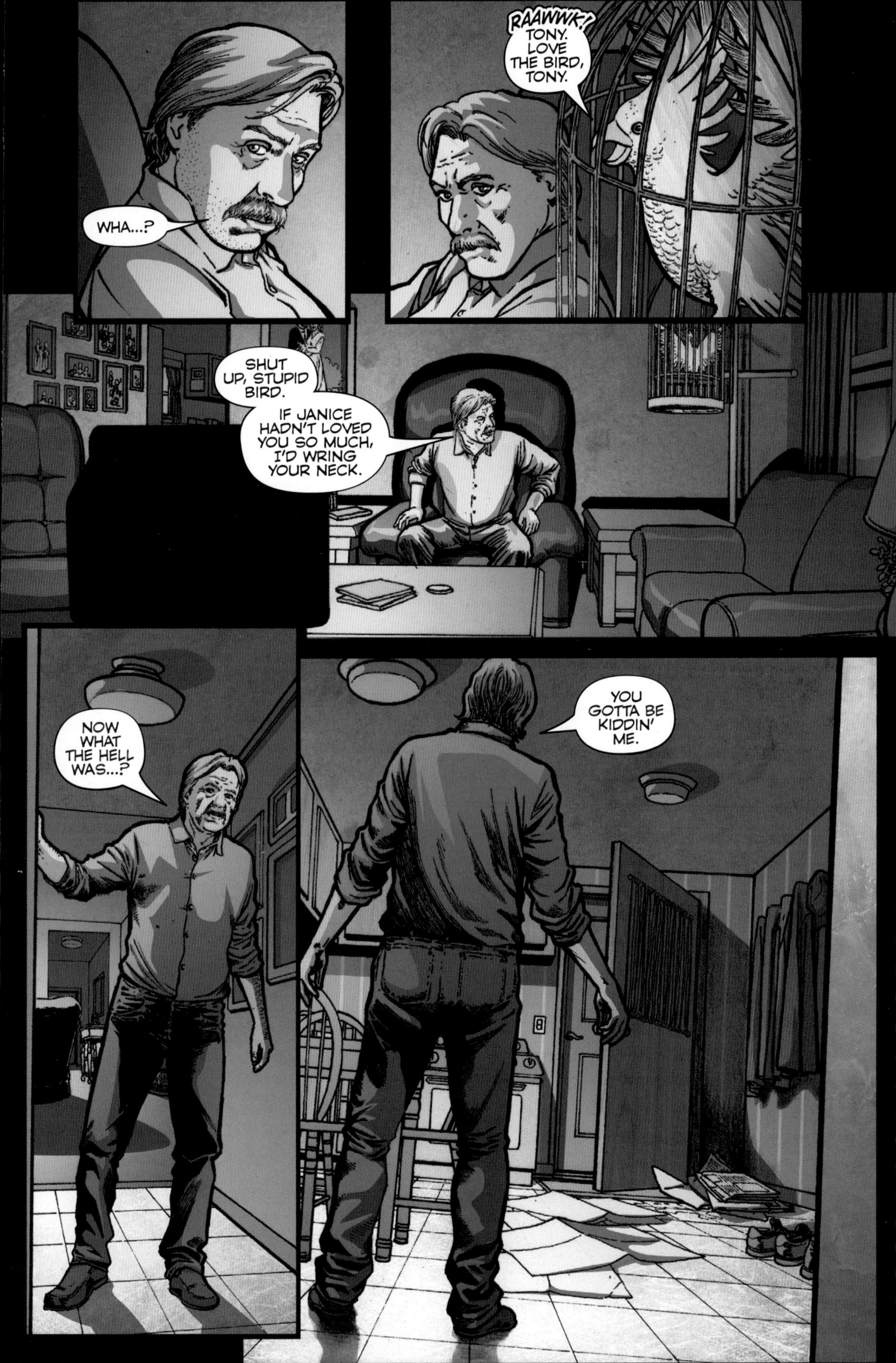
WHA...?
RAAWWK!
TONY. LOVE THE BIRD, TONY.
SHUT UP, STUPID BIRD.
IF JANICE HADN'T LOVED YOU SO MUCH, I'D WRING YOUR NECK.
NOW WHAT THE HELL WAS...?
YOU GOTTA BE KIDDIN' ME.

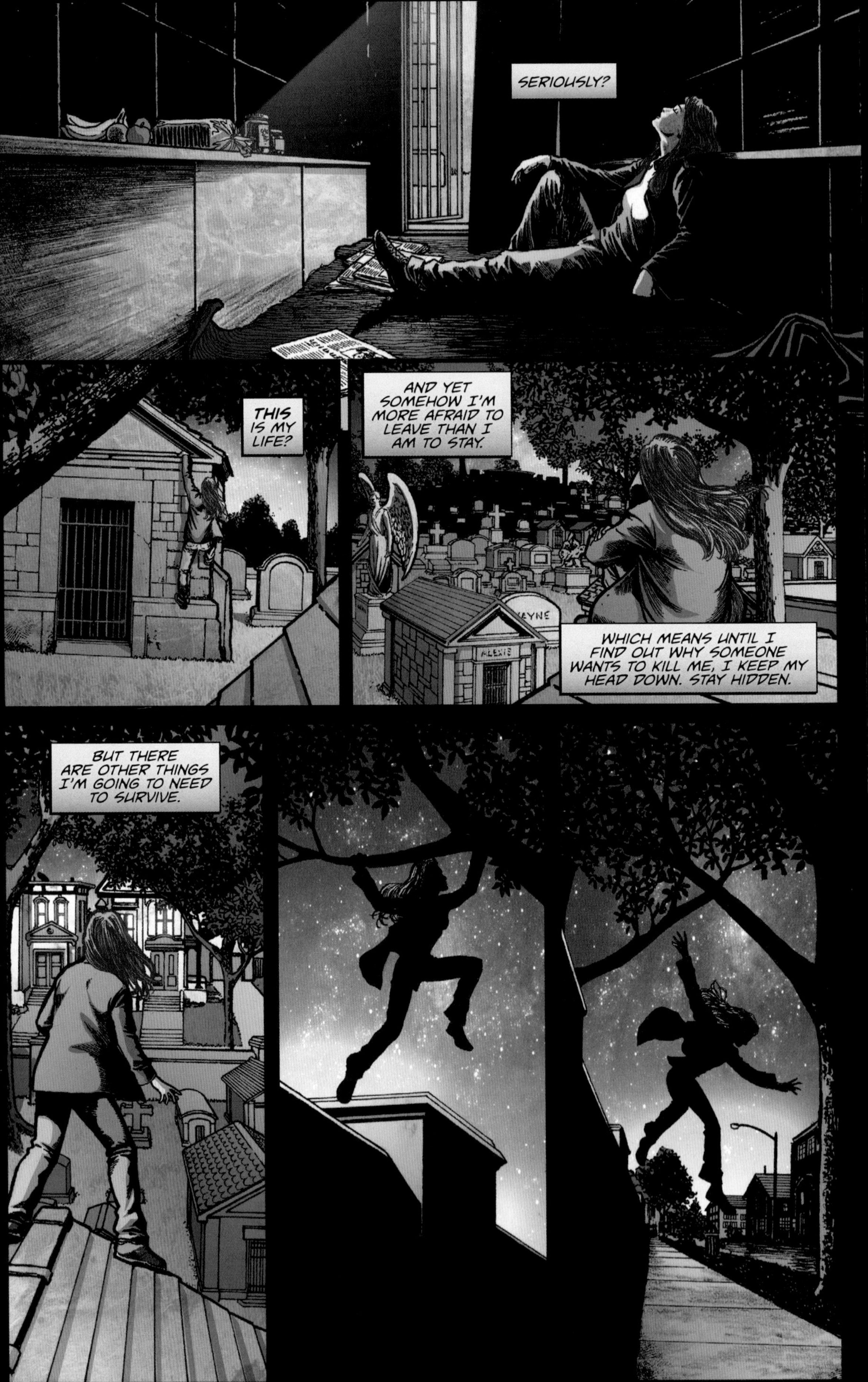
SERIOUSLY?
THIS IS MY LIFE?
AND YET SOMEHOW I'M MORE AFRAID TO LEAVE THAN I AM TO STAY.
WHICH MEANS UNTIL I FIND OUT WHY SOMEONE WANTS TO KILL ME, I KEEP MY HEAD DOWN. STAY HIDDEN.
BUT THERE ARE OTHER THINGS I'M GOING TO NEED TO SURVIVE.

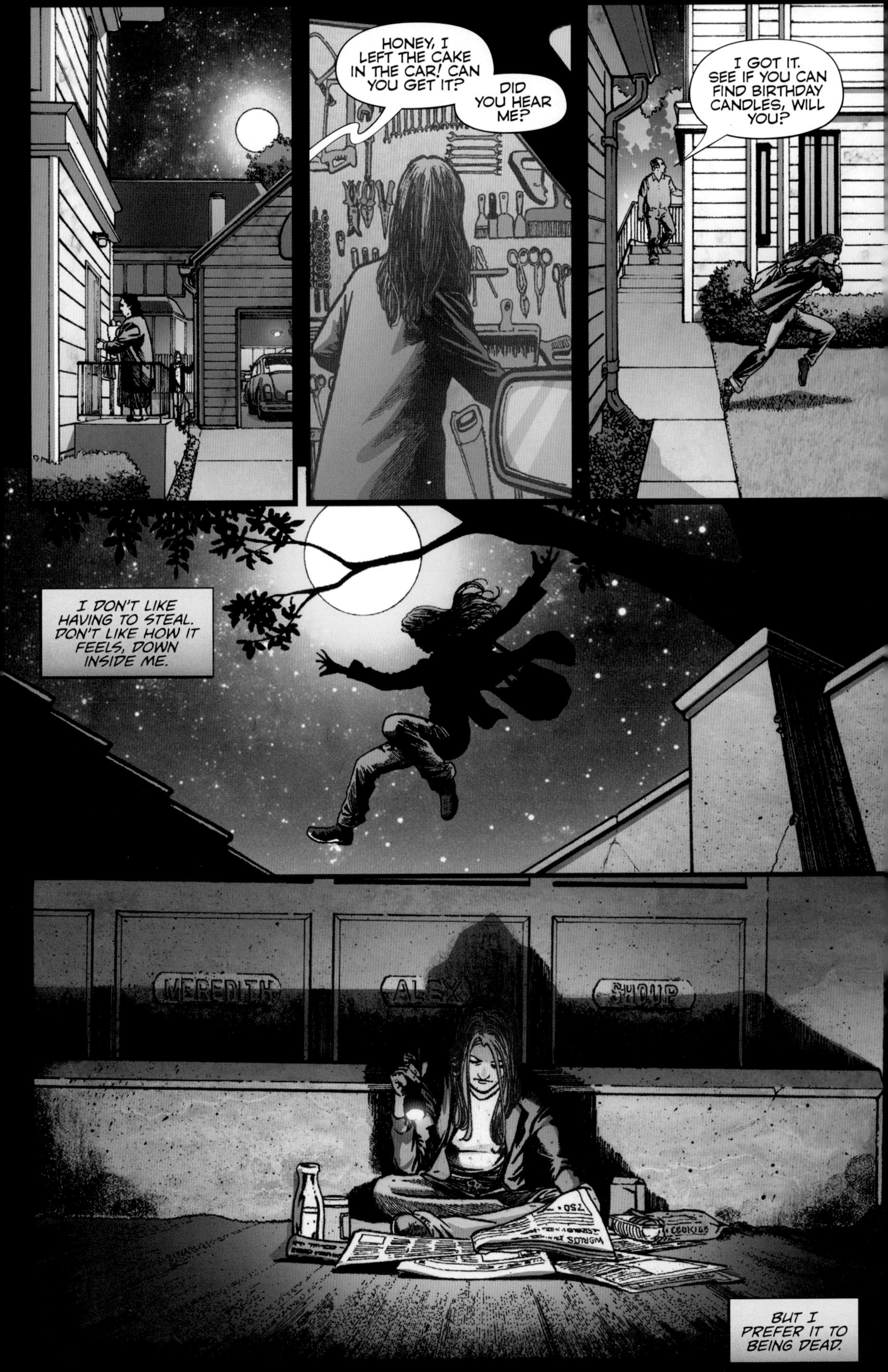
HONEY, I LEFT THE CAKE IN THE CAR! CAN YOU GET IT?
DID YOU HEAR ME?
I GOT IT. SEE IF YOU CAN FIND BIRTHDAY CANDLES, WILL YOU?
I DON'T LIKE HAVING TO STEAL. DON'T LIKE HOW IT FEELS, DOWN INSIDE ME.
MEREDITH
ALEX
SHOUP
BUT I PREFER IT TO BEING DEAD.

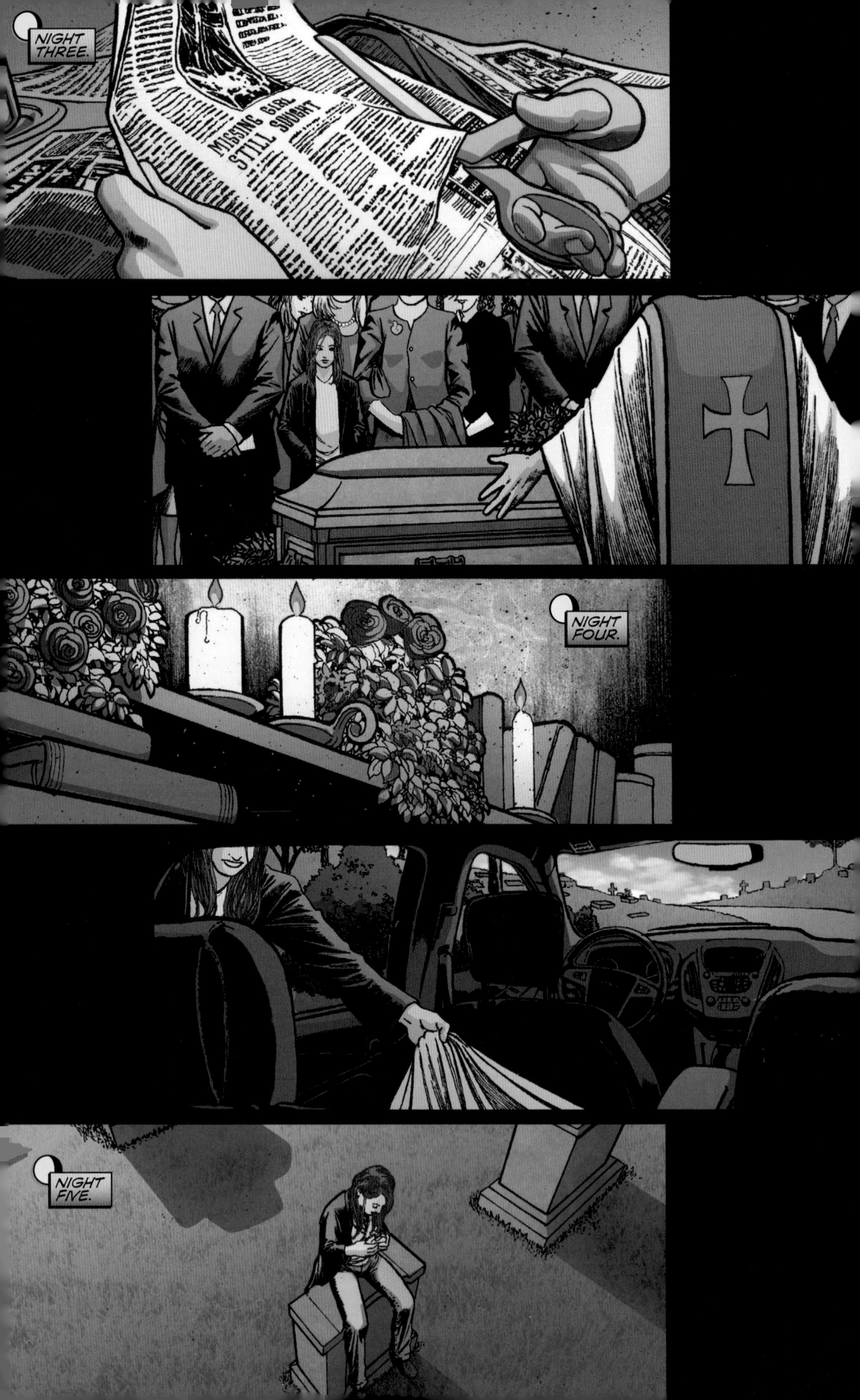
NIGHT THREE.
MISSING GIRL STILL SOUGHT
NIGHT FOUR.
NIGHT FIVE.

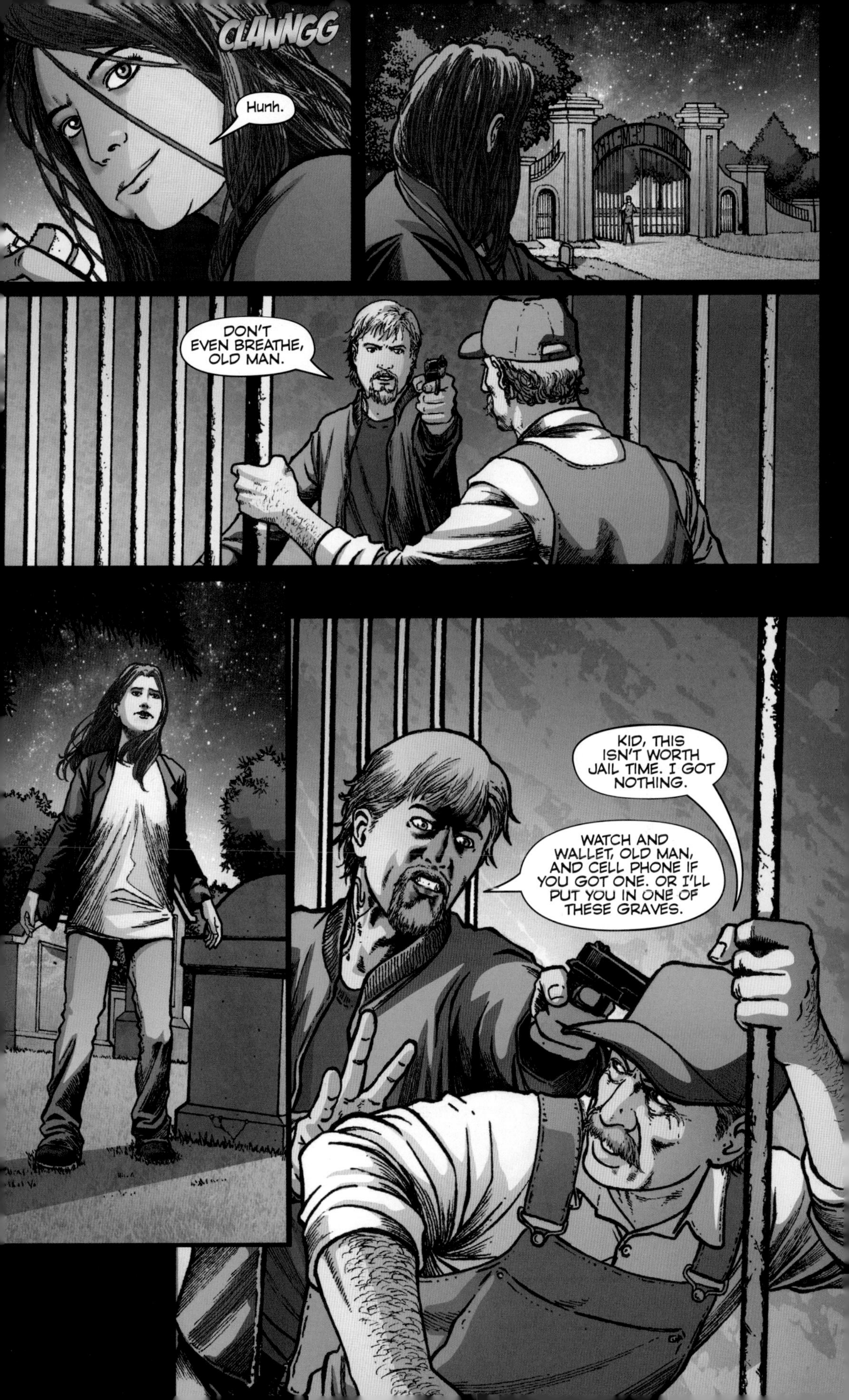
CLANNGG
Hunh.
DON'T EVEN BREATHE, OLD MAN.
KID, THIS ISN'T WORTH JAIL TIME. I GOT NOTHING.
WATCH AND WALLET, OLD MAN, AND CELL PHONE IF YOU GOT ONE. OR I'LL PUT YOU IN ONE OF THESE GRAVES.

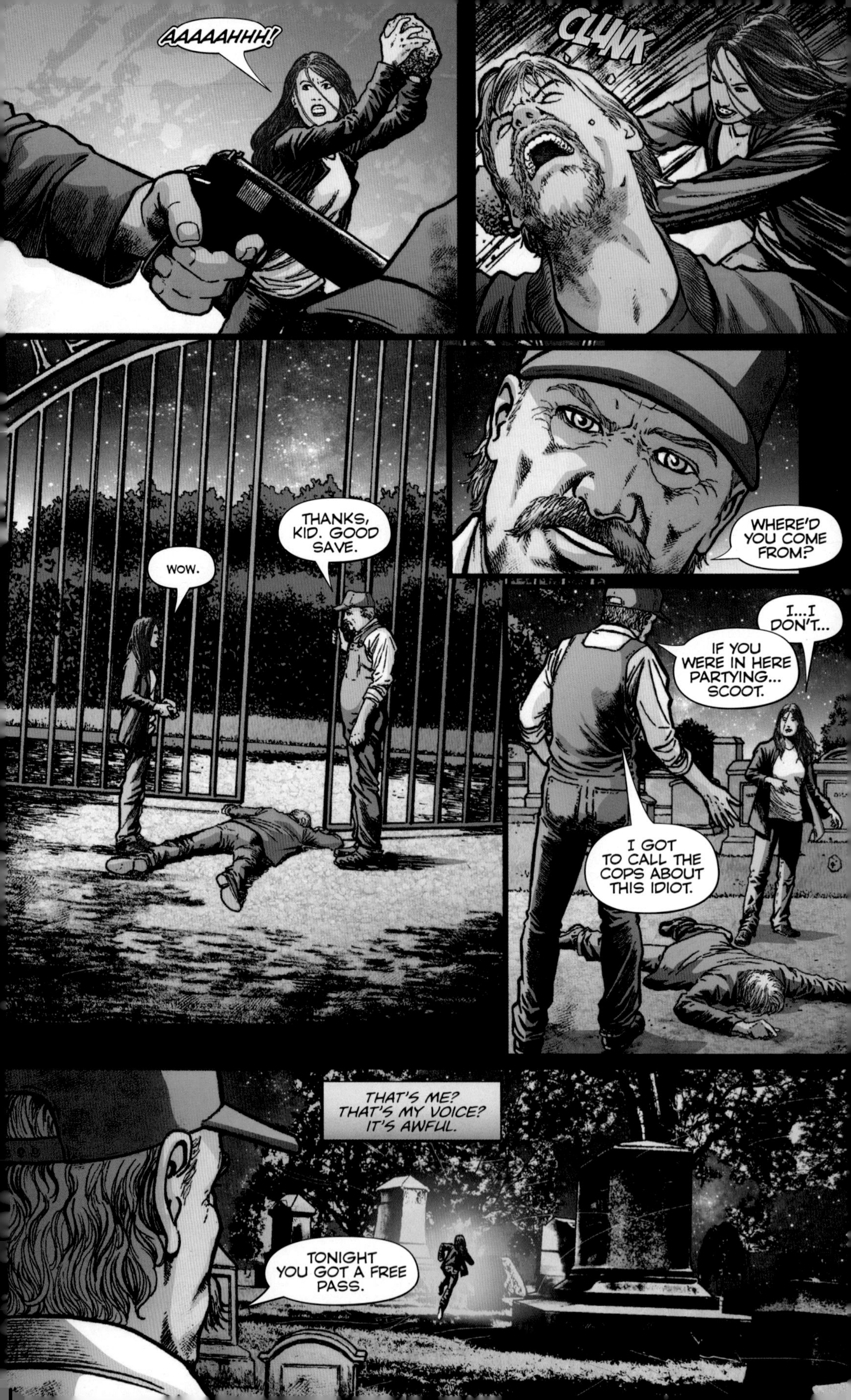
AAAAAHHH!
CLUNK
WOW.
THANKS, KID. GOOD SAVE.
WHERE'D YOU COME FROM?
I...I DON'T...
IF YOU WERE IN HERE PARTYING... SCOOT.
I GOT TO CALL THE COPS ABOUT THIS IDIOT.
THAT'S ME? THAT'S MY VOICE? IT'S AWFUL.
TONIGHT YOU GOT A FREE PASS.

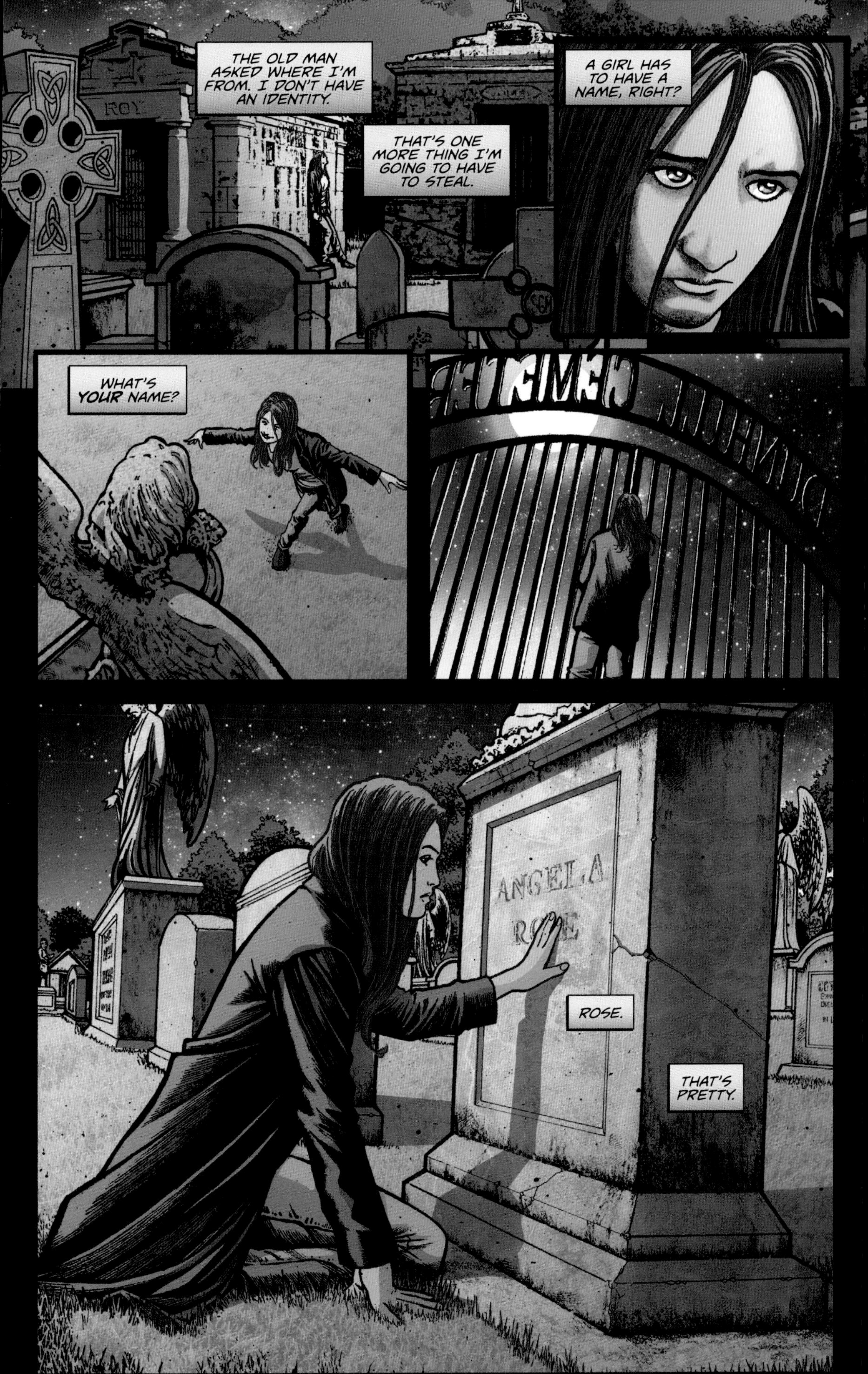

ROY
THE OLD MAN ASKED WHERE I'M FROM. I DON'T HAVE AN IDENTITY.
THAT'S ONE MORE THING I'M GOING TO HAVE TO STEAL.
A GIRL HAS TO HAVE A NAME, RIGHT?
WHAT'S YOUR NAME?
ANGELA
ROSE.
THAT'S PRETTY.

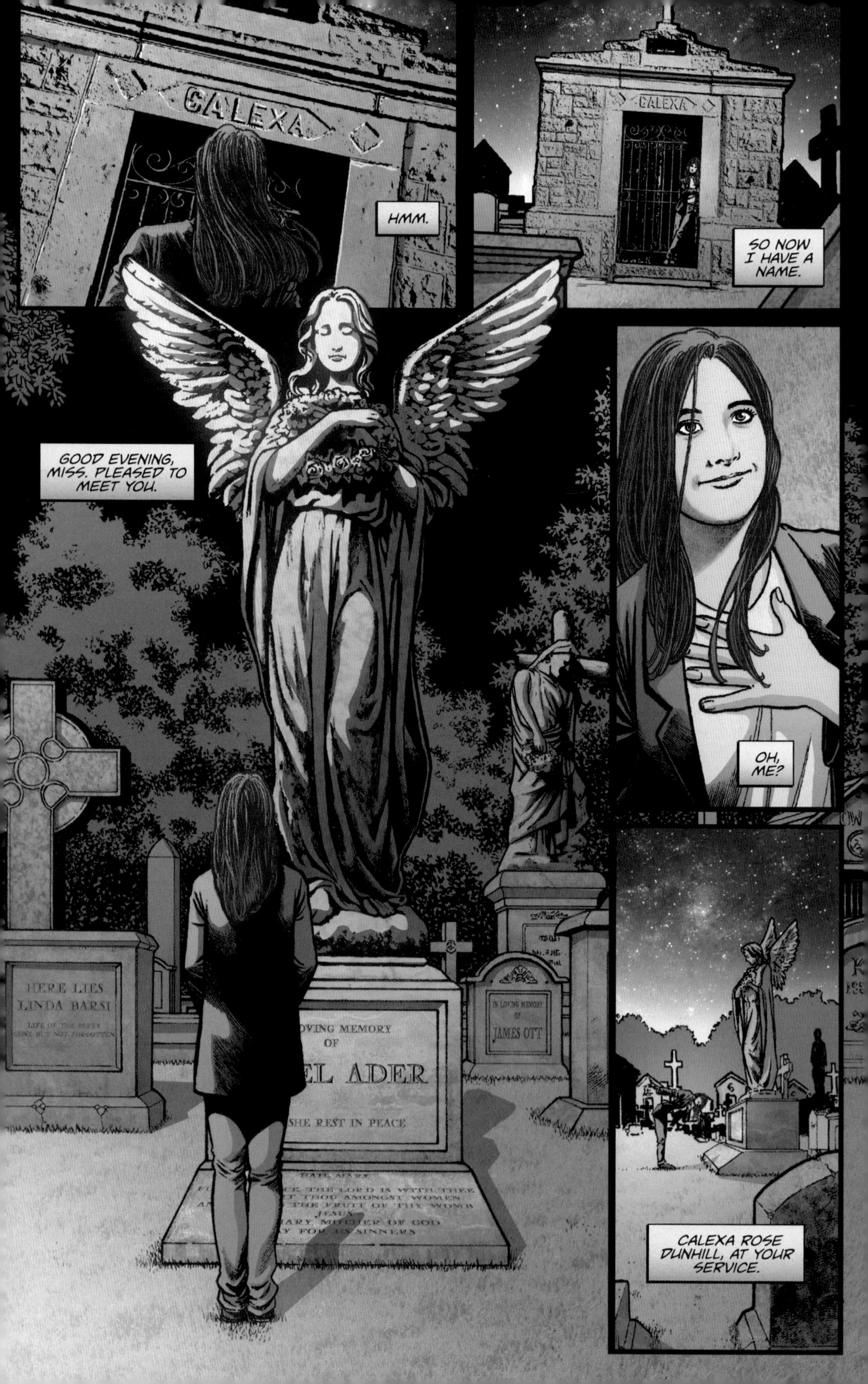
CALEXA
HMM.
CALEXA
SO NOW I HAVE A NAME.
GOOD EVENING, MISS. PLEASED TO MEET YOU.
OH, ME?
CALEXA ROSE DUNHILL, AT YOUR SERVICE.
HERE LIES LINDA BARSI
LOVING MEMORY OF
EL ADER
SHE REST IN PEACE
IN LOVING MEMORY OF
JAMES OTT

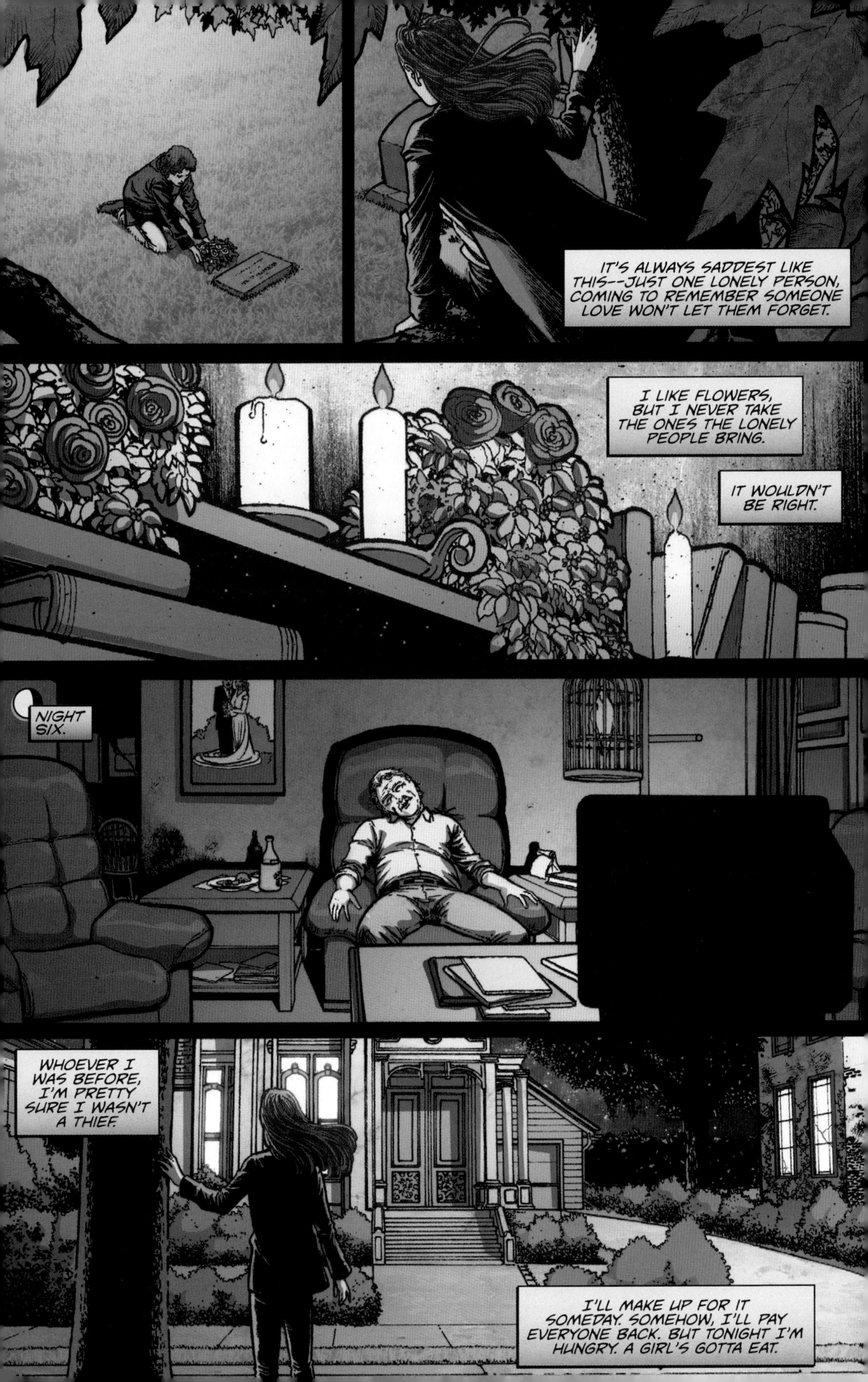
IT'S ALWAYS SADDEST LIKE THIS--JUST ONE LONELY PERSON, COMING TO REMEMBER SOMEONE LOVE WON'T LET THEM FORGET.
I LIKE FLOWERS, BUT I NEVER TAKE THE ONES THE LONELY PEOPLE BRING.
IT WOULDN'T BE RIGHT.
NIGHT SIX.
WHOEVER I WAS BEFORE, I'M PRETTY SURE I WASN'T A THIEF.
I'LL MAKE UP FOR IT SOMEDAY. SOMEHOW, I'LL PAY EVERYONE BACK. BUT TONIGHT I'M HUNGRY. A GIRL'S GOTTA EAT.

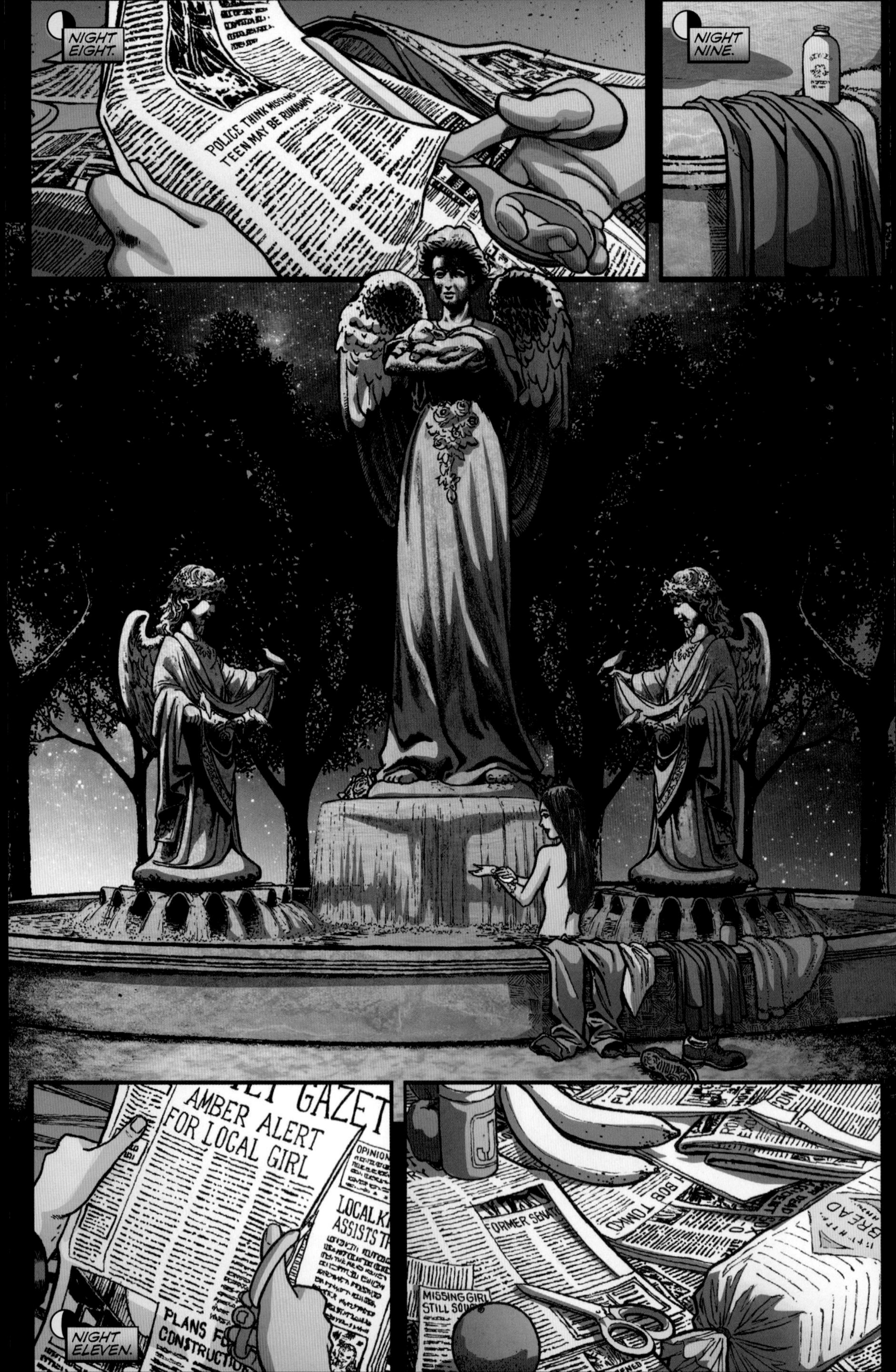
NIGHT EIGHT.
POLICE THINK MISSING TEEN MAY BE RUNAWAY
NIGHT NINE.
AMBER ALERT FOR LOCAL GIRL
NIGHT ELEVEN.

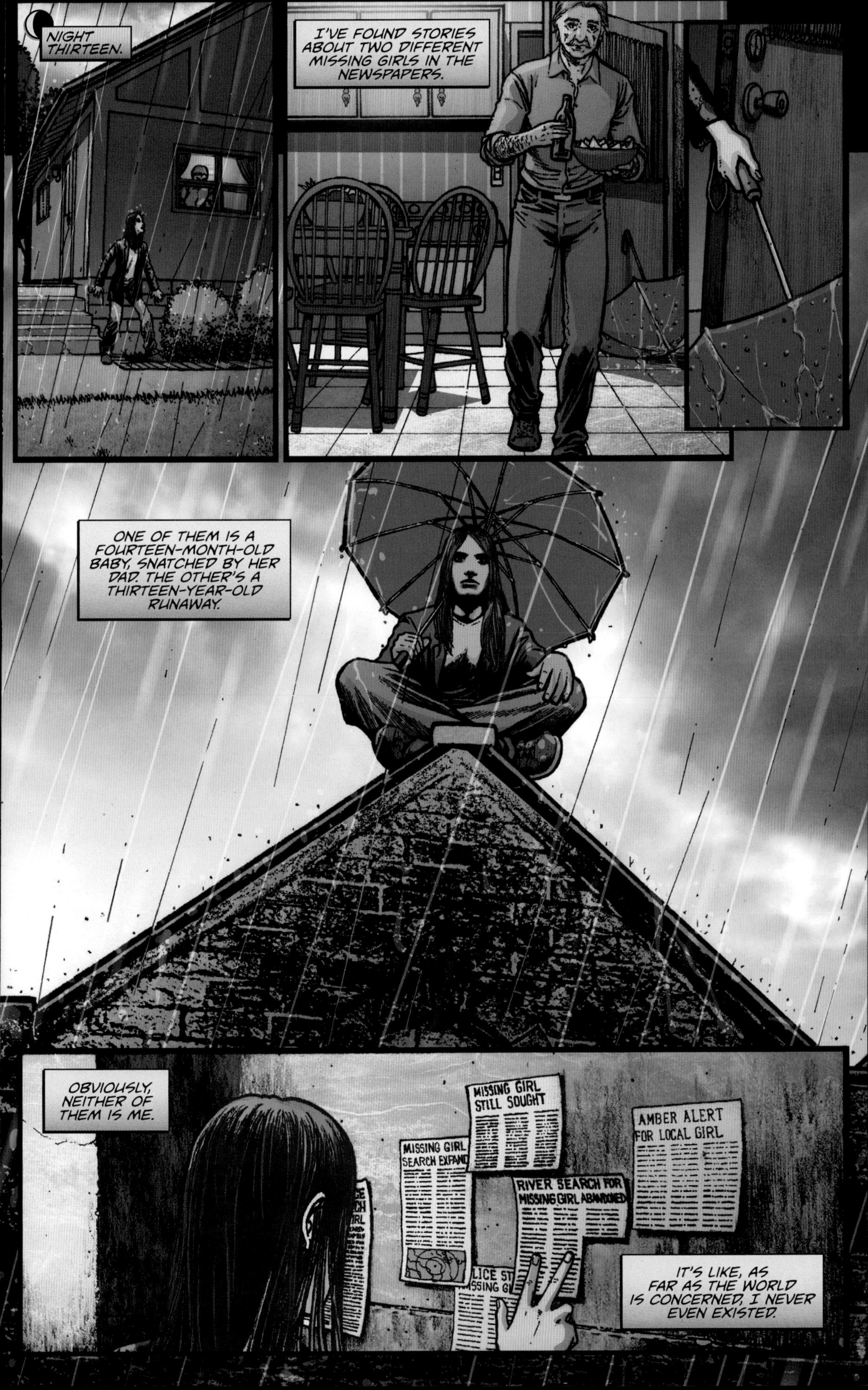
NIGHT THIRTEEN.
I'VE FOUND STORIES ABOUT TWO DIFFERENT MISSING GIRLS IN THE NEWSPAPERS.
ONE OF THEM IS A FOURTEEN-MONTH-OLD BABY, SNATCHED BY HER DAD. THE OTHER'S A THIRTEEN-YEAR-OLD RUNAWAY.
OBVIOUSLY, NEITHER OF THEM IS ME.
MISSING GIRL STILL SOUGHT
AMBER ALERT FOR LOCAL GIRL
MISSING GIRL SEARCH EXPAND
RIVER SEARCH FOR MISSING GIRL ABANDONED
IT'S LIKE, AS FAR AS THE WORLD IS CONCERNED, I NEVER EVEN EXISTED.

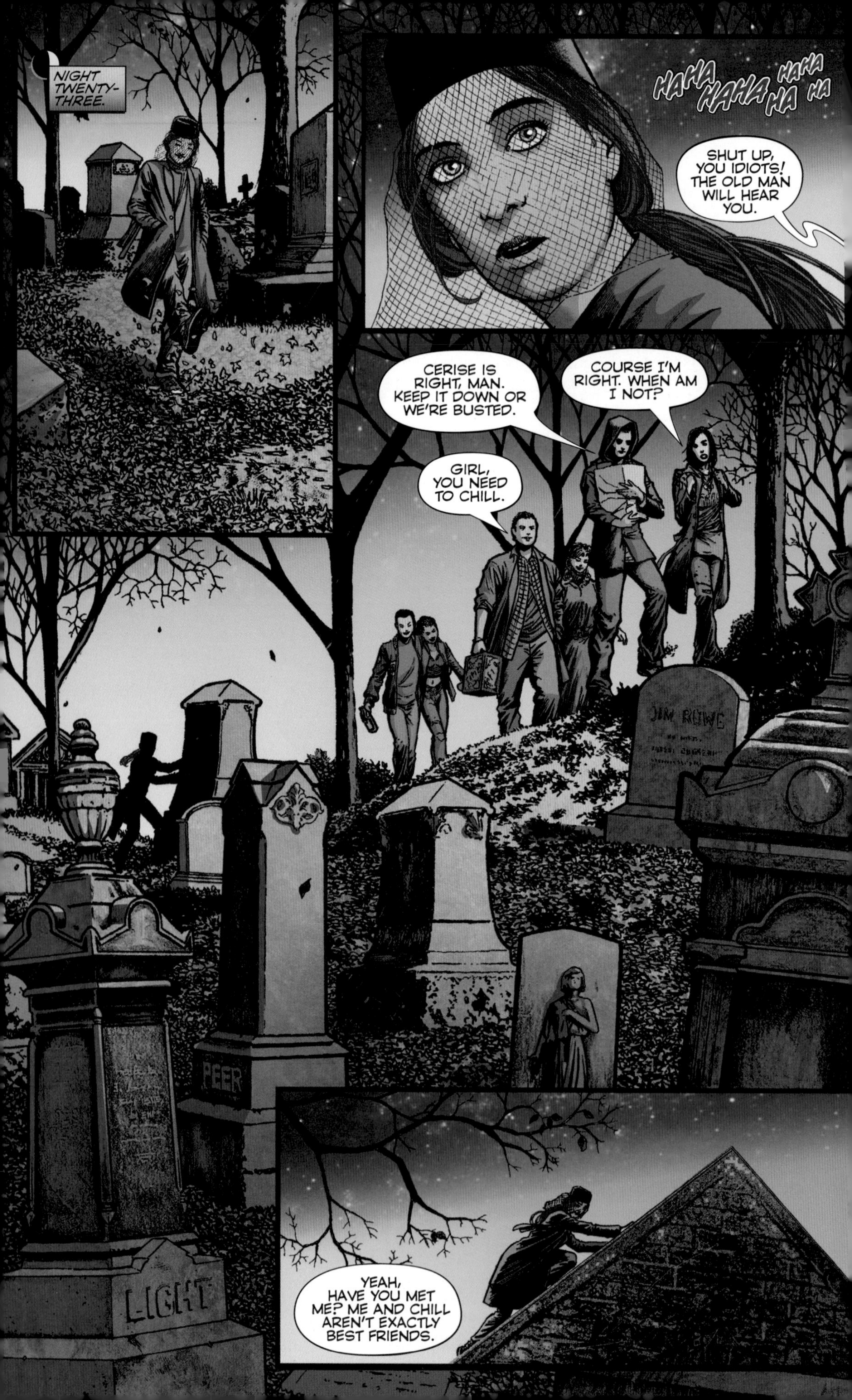

NIGHT TWENTY-THREE.
HAHA HAHA HAHA HA HA
SHUT UP, YOU IDIOTS! THE OLD MAN WILL HEAR YOU.
CERISE IS RIGHT, MAN. KEEP IT DOWN OR WE'RE BUSTED.
COURSE I'M RIGHT. WHEN AM I NOT?
GIRL, YOU NEED TO CHILL.
JIM ROWE
PEER
LIGHT
YEAH, HAVE YOU MET ME? ME AND CHILL AREN'T EXACTLY BEST FRIENDS.

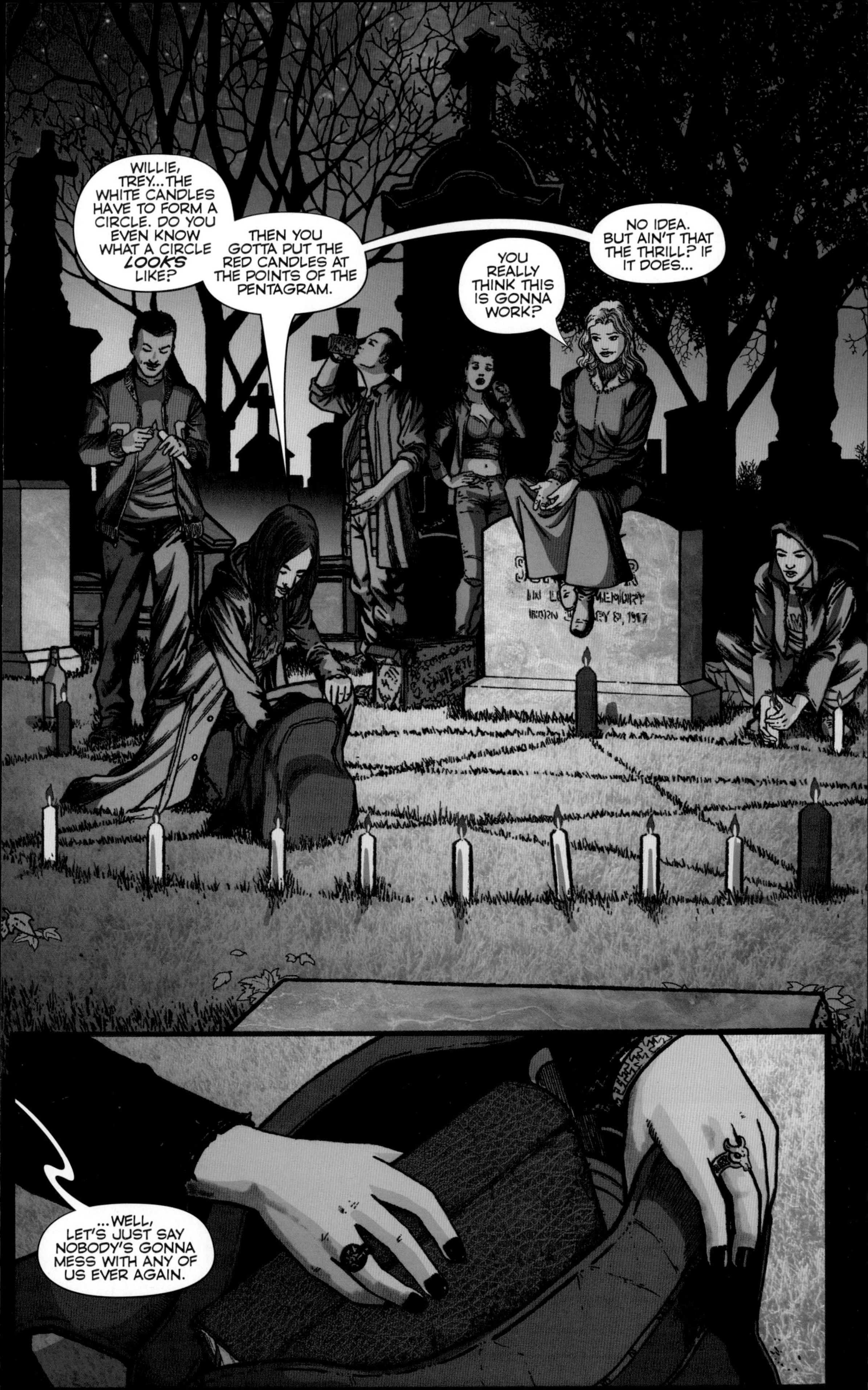
WILLIE, TREY...THE WHITE CANDLES HAVE TO FORM A CIRCLE. DO YOU EVEN KNOW WHAT A CIRCLE *LOOKS* LIKE?
THEN YOU GOTTA PUT THE RED CANDLES AT THE POINTS OF THE PENTAGRAM.
YOU REALLY THINK THIS IS GONNA WORK?
NO IDEA. BUT AIN'T THAT THE THRILL? IF IT DOES...
...WELL, LET'S JUST SAY NOBODY'S GONNA MESS WITH ANY OF US EVER AGAIN.

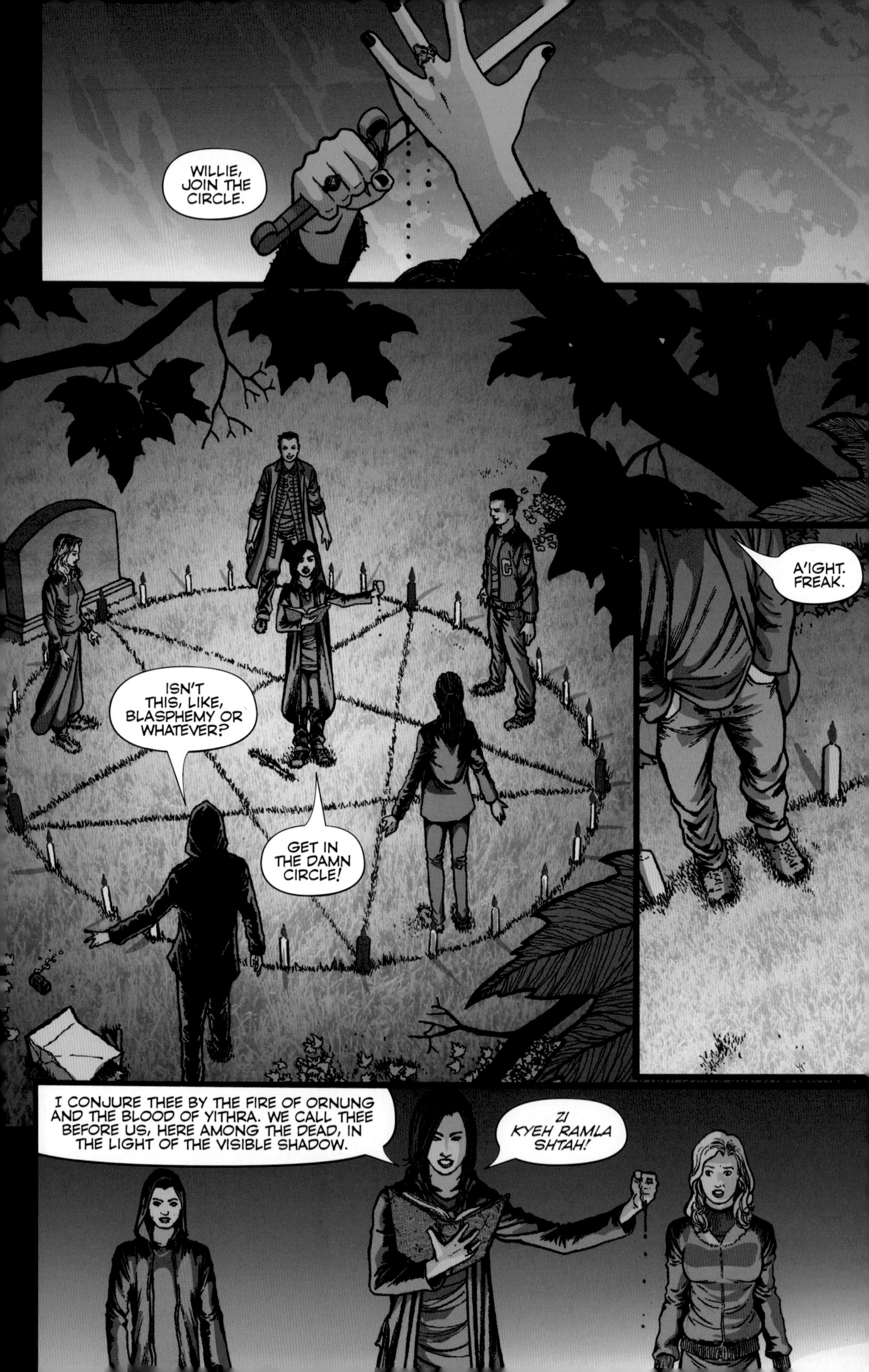
WILLIE, JOIN THE CIRCLE.
A'IGHT. FREAK.
ISN'T THIS, LIKE, BLASPHEMY OR WHATEVER?
GET IN THE DAMN CIRCLE!
I CONJURE THEE BY THE FIRE OF ORNUNG AND THE BLOOD OF YITHRA. WE CALL THEE BEFORE US, HERE AMONG THE DEAD, IN THE LIGHT OF THE VISIBLE SHADOW.
ZI KYEH RAMLA SHTAH!

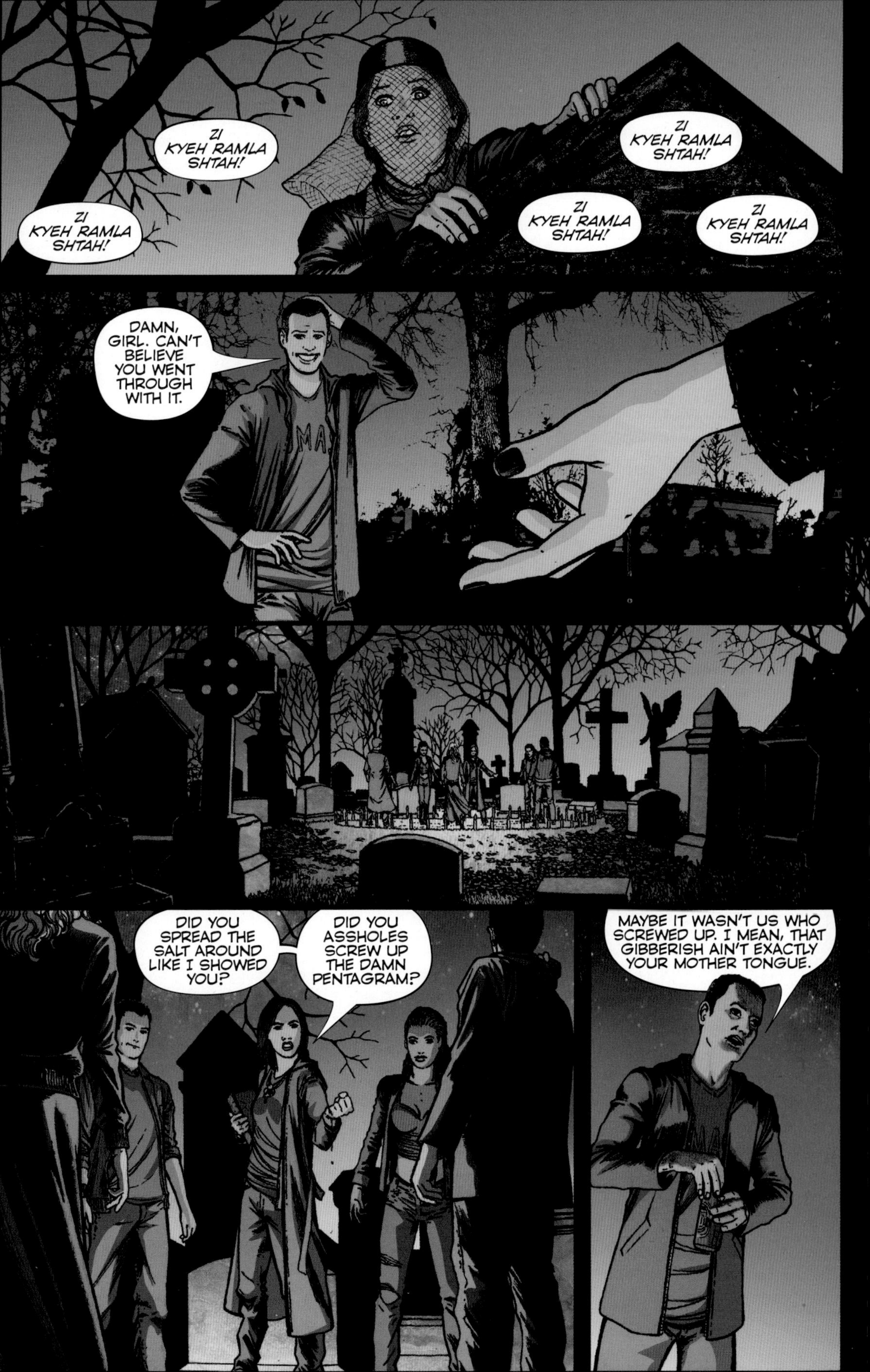
ZI KYEH RAMLA SHTAH!
ZI KYEH RAMLA SHTAH!
ZI KYEH RAMLA SHTAH!
ZI KYEH RAMLA SHTAH!
ZI KYEH RAMLA SHTAH!
DAMN, GIRL. CAN'T BELIEVE YOU WENT THROUGH WITH IT.
DID YOU SPREAD THE SALT AROUND LIKE I SHOWED YOU?
DID YOU ASSHOLES SCREW UP THE DAMN PENTAGRAM?
MAYBE IT WASN'T US WHO SCREWED UP. I MEAN, THAT GIBBERISH AIN'T EXACTLY YOUR MOTHER TONGUE.

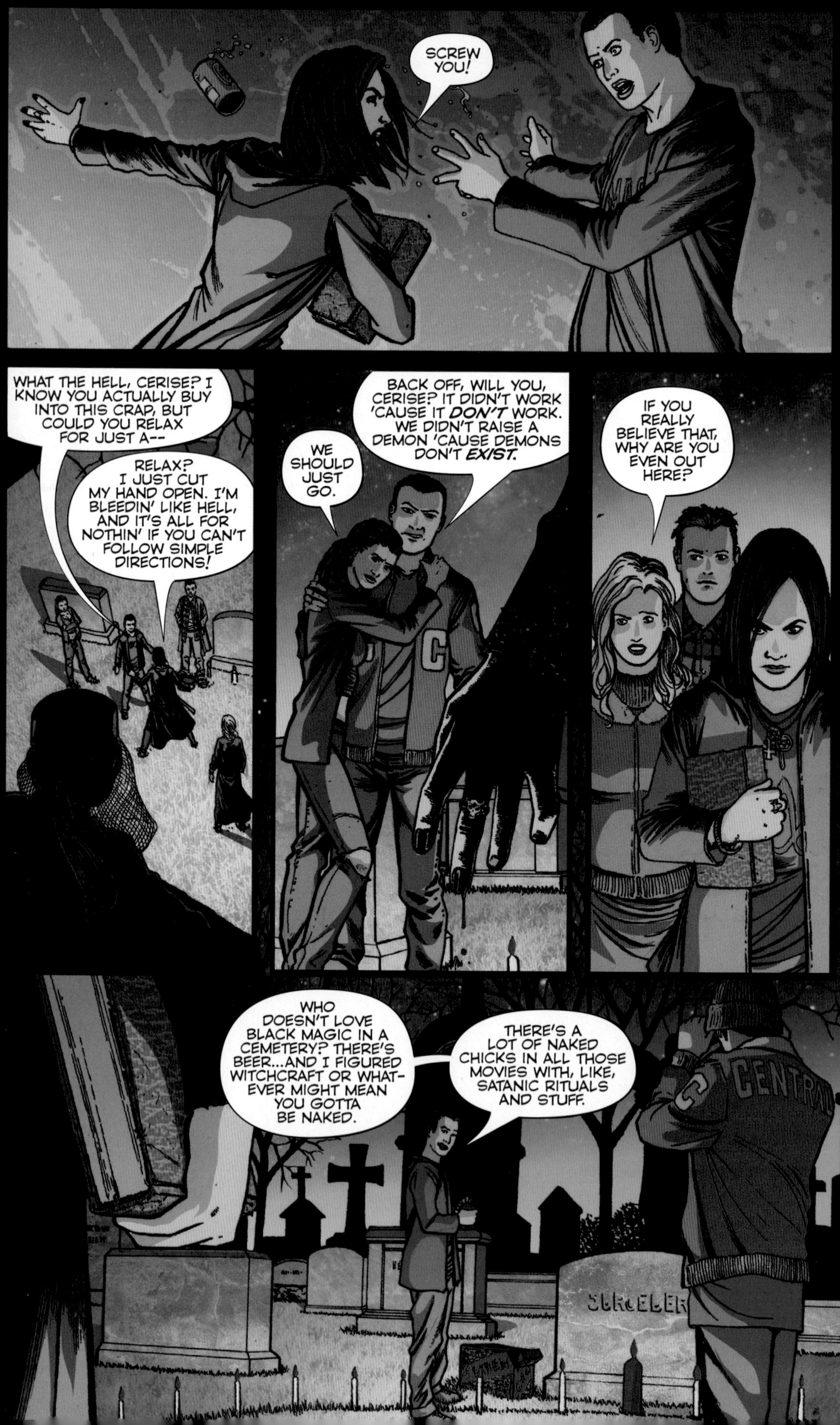
SCREW YOU!
WHAT THE HELL, CERISE? I KNOW YOU ACTUALLY BUY INTO THIS CRAP, BUT COULD YOU RELAX FOR JUST A--
RELAX? I JUST CUT MY HAND OPEN. I'M BLEEDIN' LIKE HELL, AND IT'S ALL FOR NOTHIN' IF YOU CAN'T FOLLOW SIMPLE DIRECTIONS!
WE SHOULD JUST GO.
BACK OFF, WILL YOU, CERISE? IT DIDN'T WORK 'CAUSE IT DON'T WORK. WE DIDN'T RAISE A DEMON 'CAUSE DEMONS DON'T EXIST.
IF YOU REALLY BELIEVE THAT, WHY ARE YOU EVEN OUT HERE?
WHO DOESN'T LOVE BLACK MAGIC IN A CEMETERY? THERE'S BEER...AND I FIGURED WITCHCRAFT OR WHAT-EVER MIGHT MEAN YOU GOTTA BE NAKED.
THERE'S A LOT OF NAKED CHICKS IN ALL THOSE MOVIES WITH, LIKE, SATANIC RITUALS AND STUFF.
CENTRAL

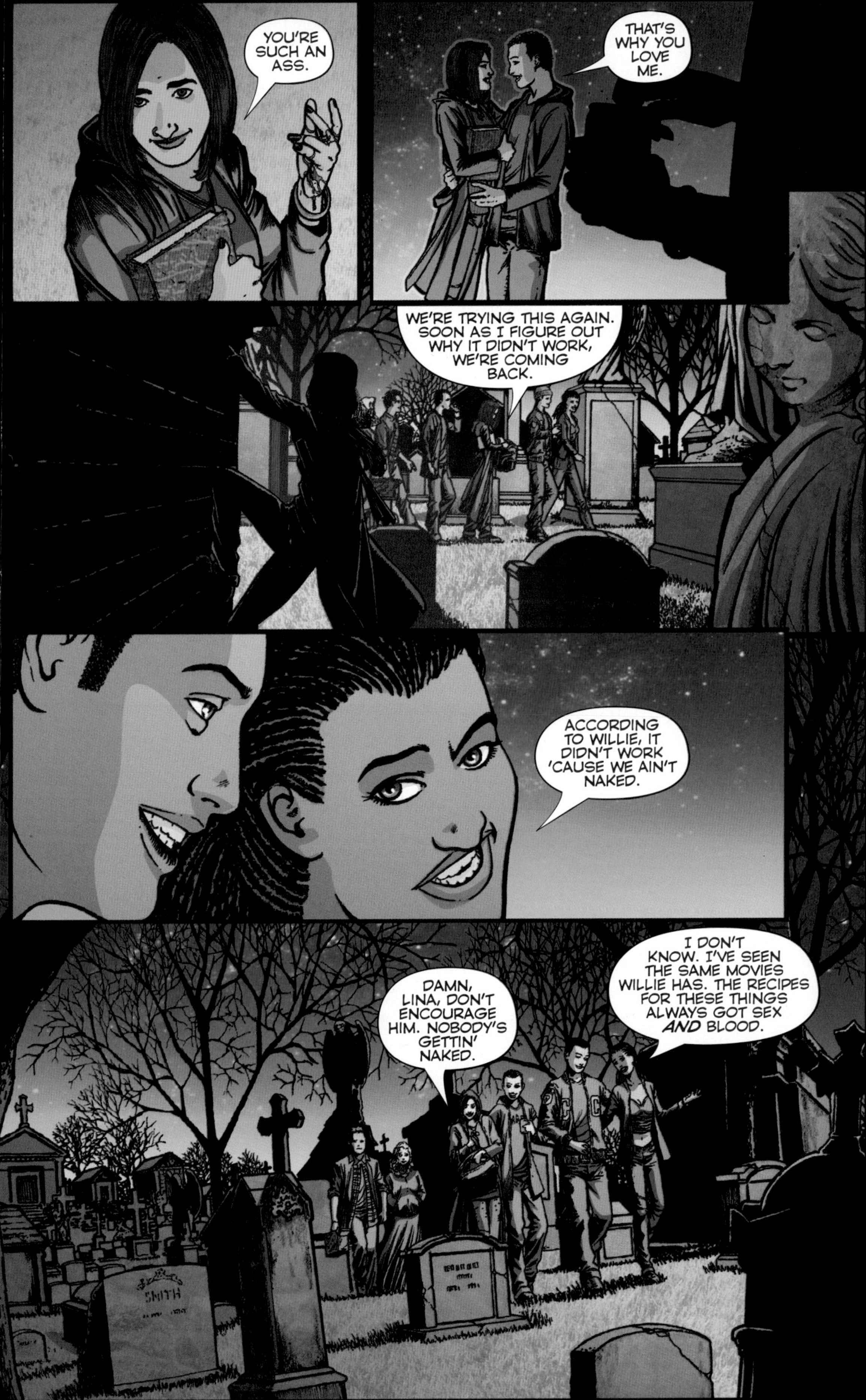
YOU'RE SUCH AN ASS.
THAT'S WHY YOU LOVE ME.
WE'RE TRYING THIS AGAIN. SOON AS I FIGURE OUT WHY IT DIDN'T WORK, WE'RE COMING BACK.
ACCORDING TO WILLIE, IT DIDN'T WORK 'CAUSE WE AIN'T NAKED.
DAMN, LINA, DON'T ENCOURAGE HIM. NOBODY'S GETTIN' NAKED.
I DON'T KNOW. I'VE SEEN THE SAME MOVIES WILLIE HAS. THE RECIPES FOR THESE THINGS ALWAYS GOT SEX *AND* BLOOD.
SMITH

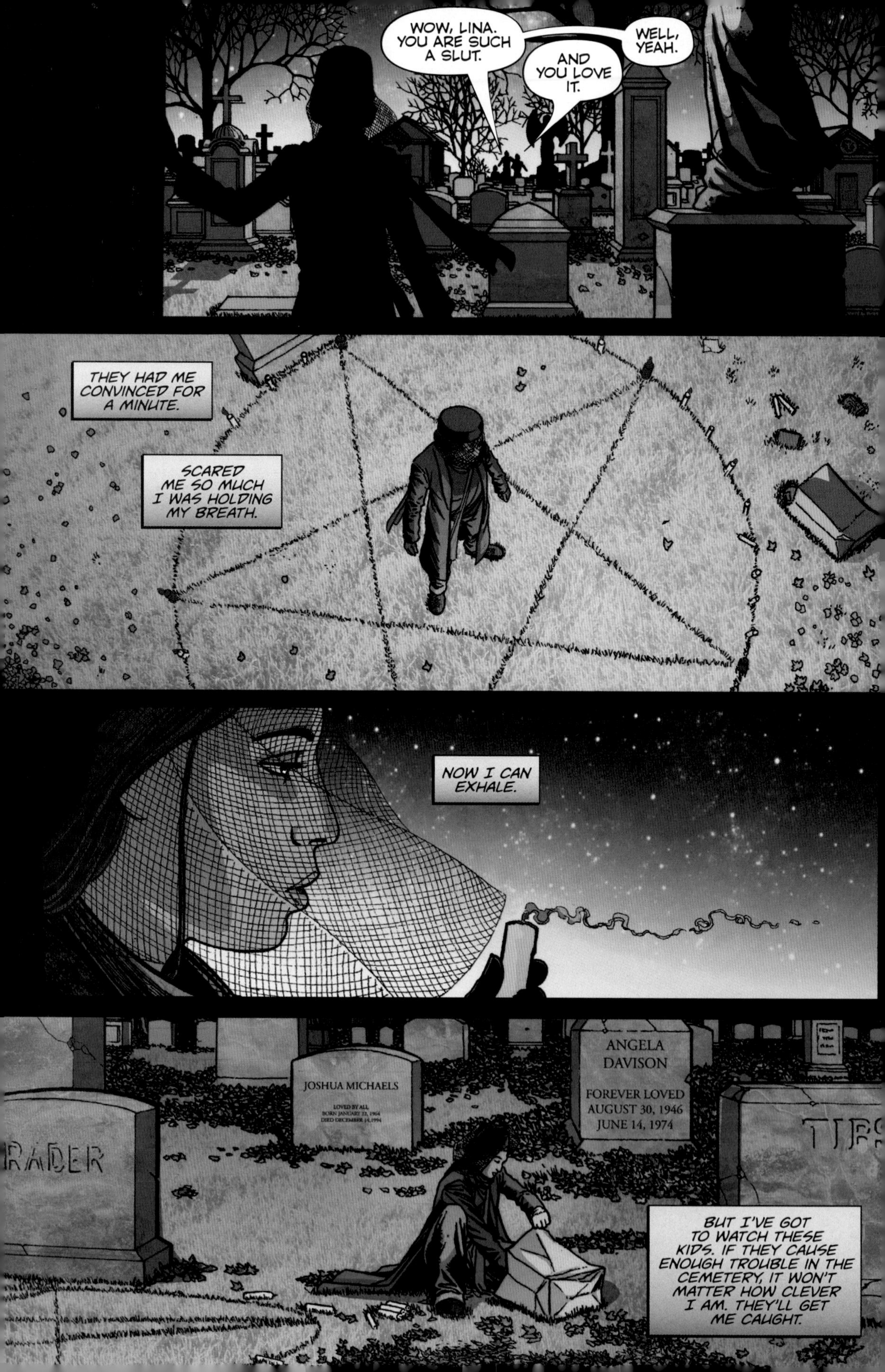

WOW, LINA. YOU ARE SUCH A SLUT.
WELL, YEAH.
AND YOU LOVE IT.
THEY HAD ME CONVINCED FOR A MINUTE.
SCARED ME SO MUCH I WAS HOLDING MY BREATH.
NOW I CAN EXHALE.
JOSHUA MICHAELS
ANGELA DAVISON
FOREVER LOVED
AUGUST 30, 1946
JUNE 14, 1974
RADER
BUT I'VE GOT TO WATCH THESE KIDS. IF THEY CAUSE ENOUGH TROUBLE IN THE CEMETERY, IT WON'T MATTER HOW CLEVER I AM. THEY'LL GET ME CAUGHT.

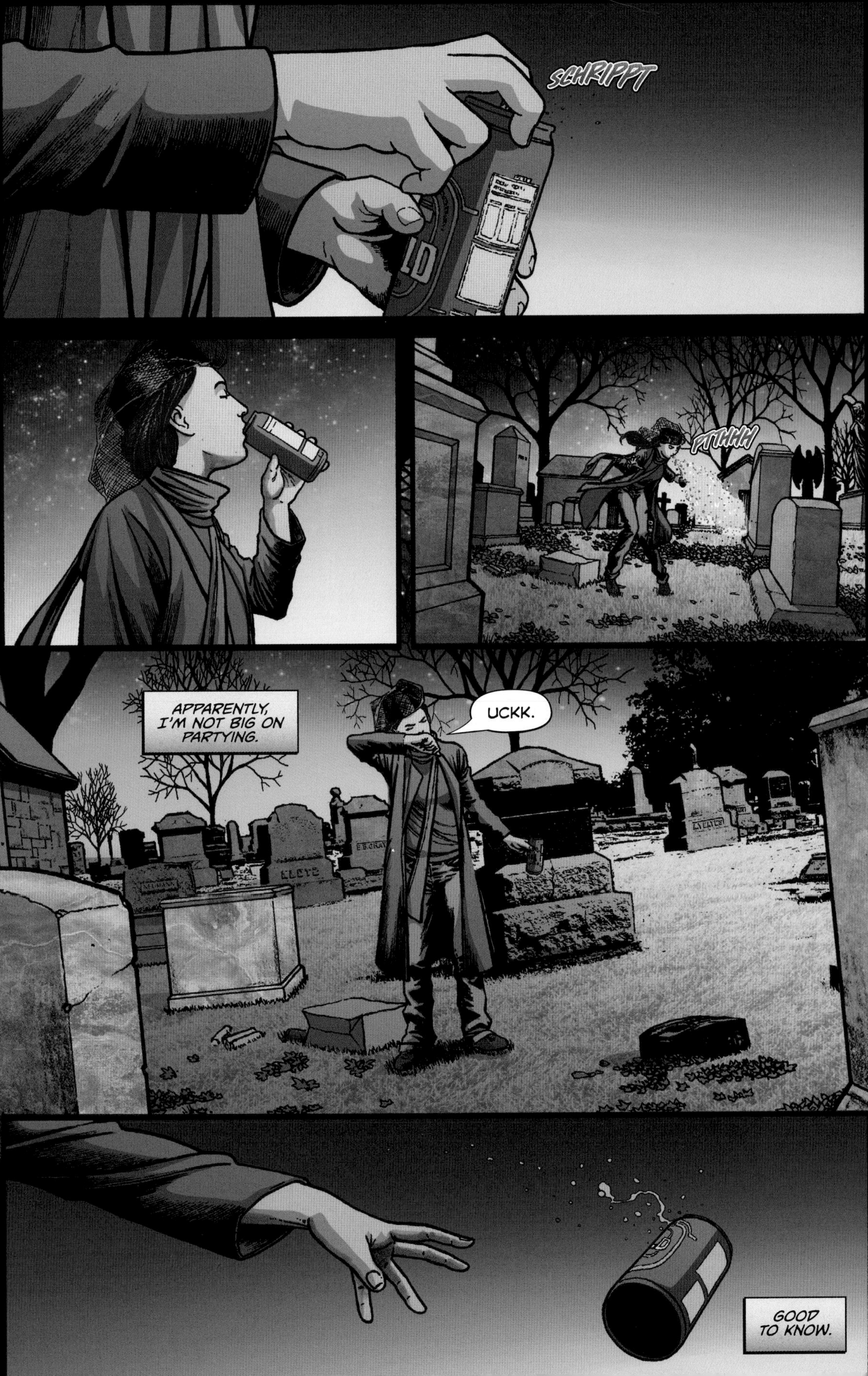
SCHRIPPT
PTTHHH
APPARENTLY, I'M NOT BIG ON PARTYING.
UCKK.
GOOD TO KNOW.

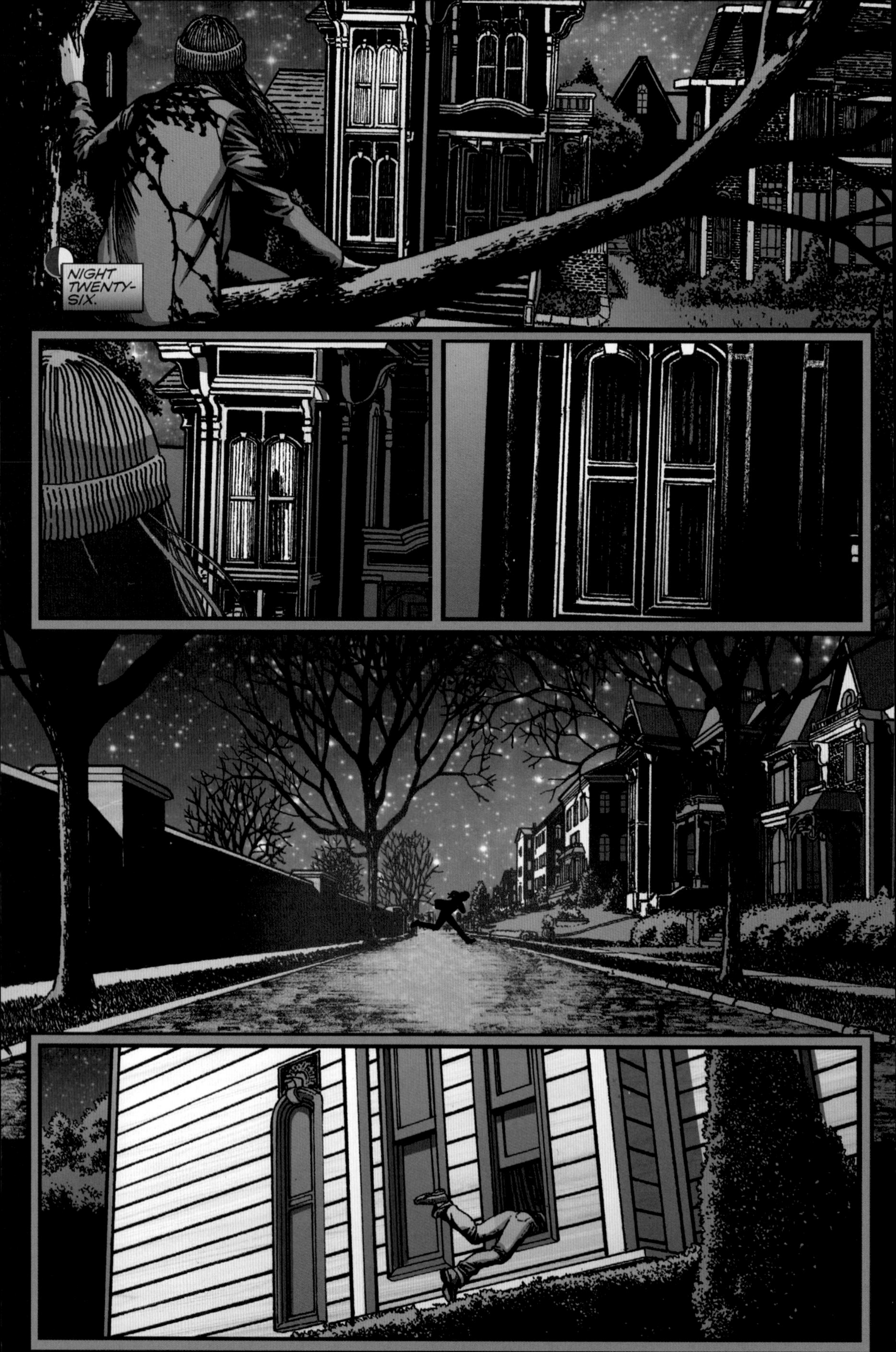

NIGHT TWENTY-SIX.

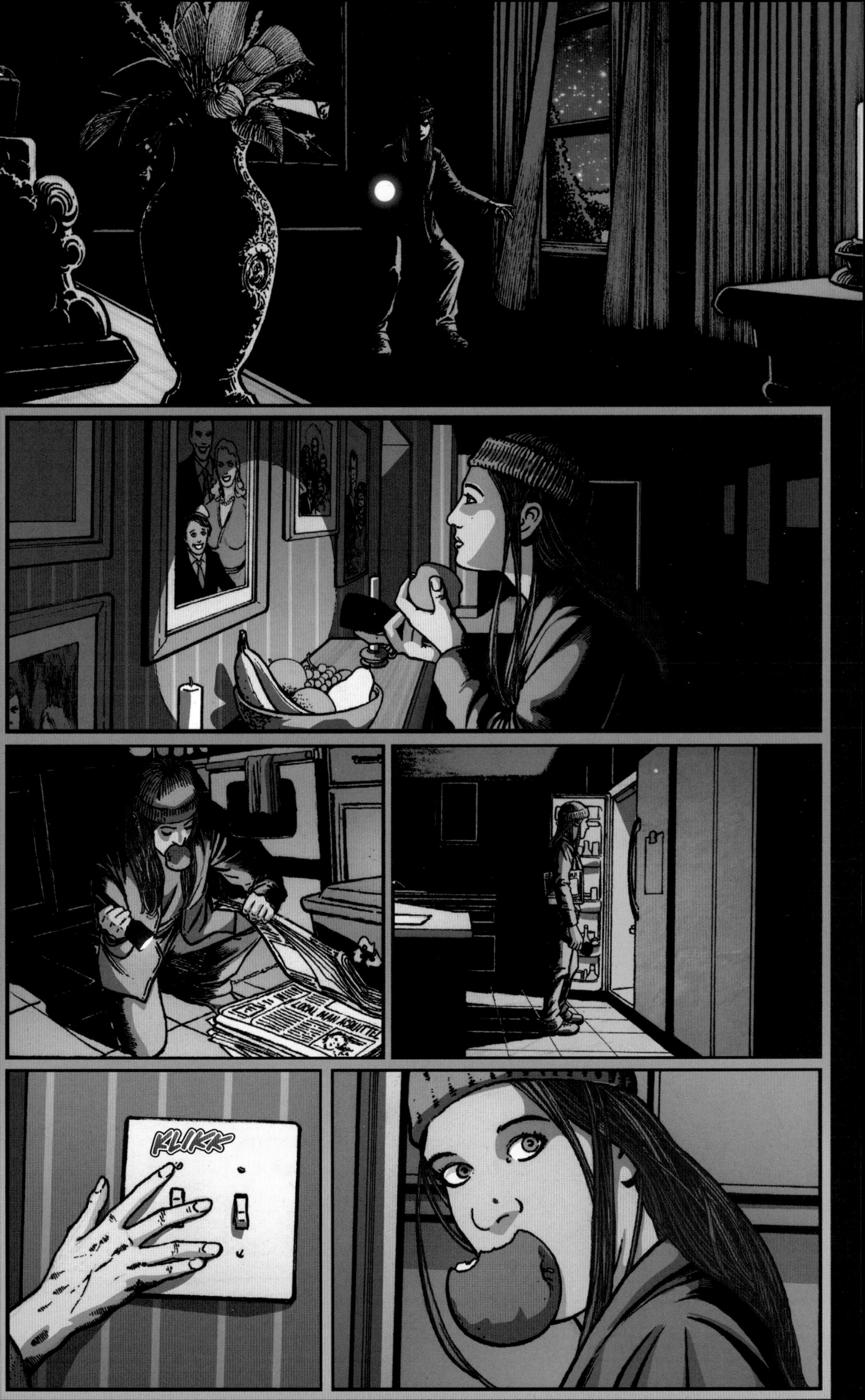
LOCAL MAN ACQUITTE
KLIKK

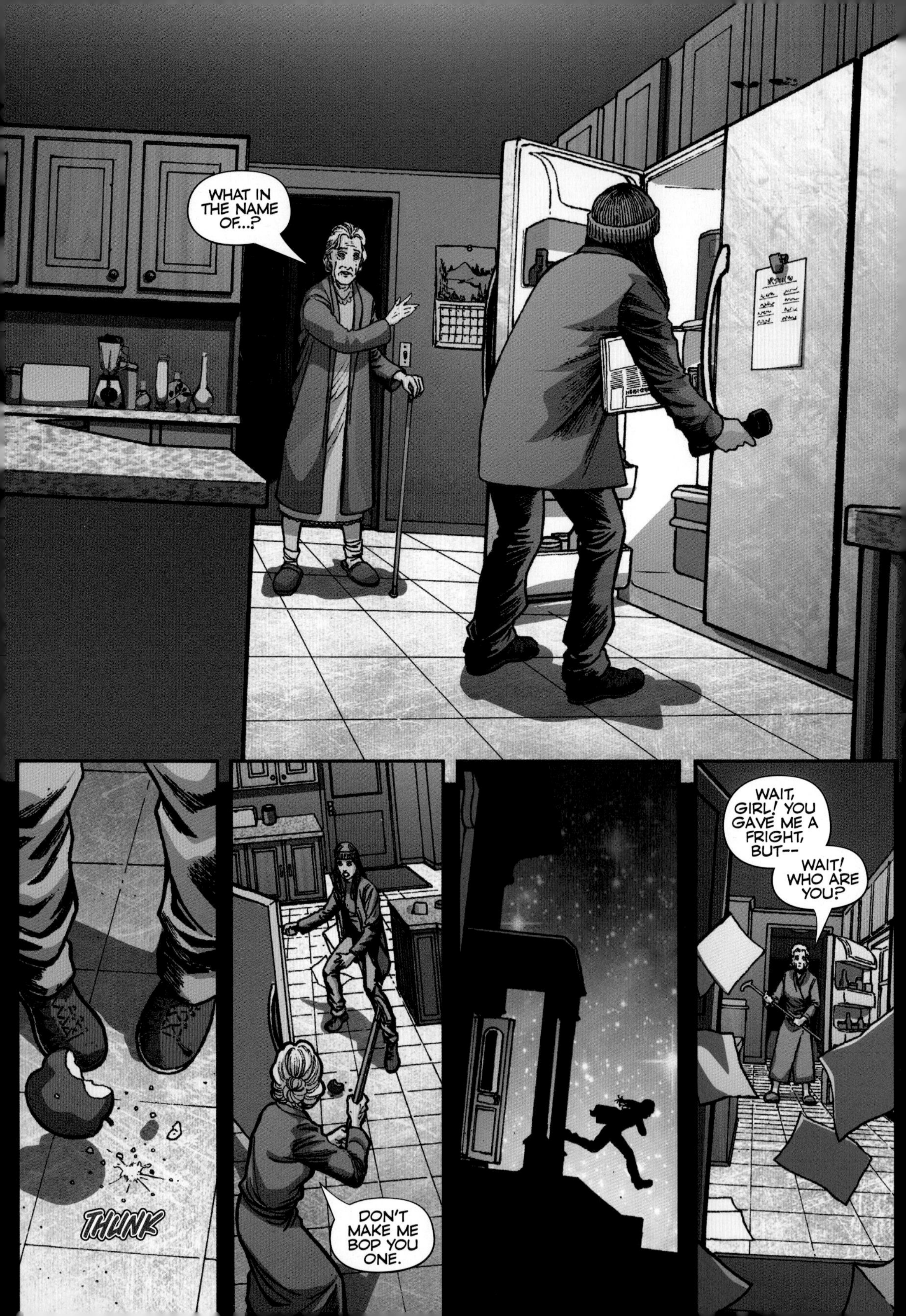
WHAT IN THE NAME OF...?
THUNK
DON'T MAKE ME BOP YOU ONE.
WAIT, GIRL! YOU GAVE ME A FRIGHT, BUT--
WAIT! WHO ARE YOU?

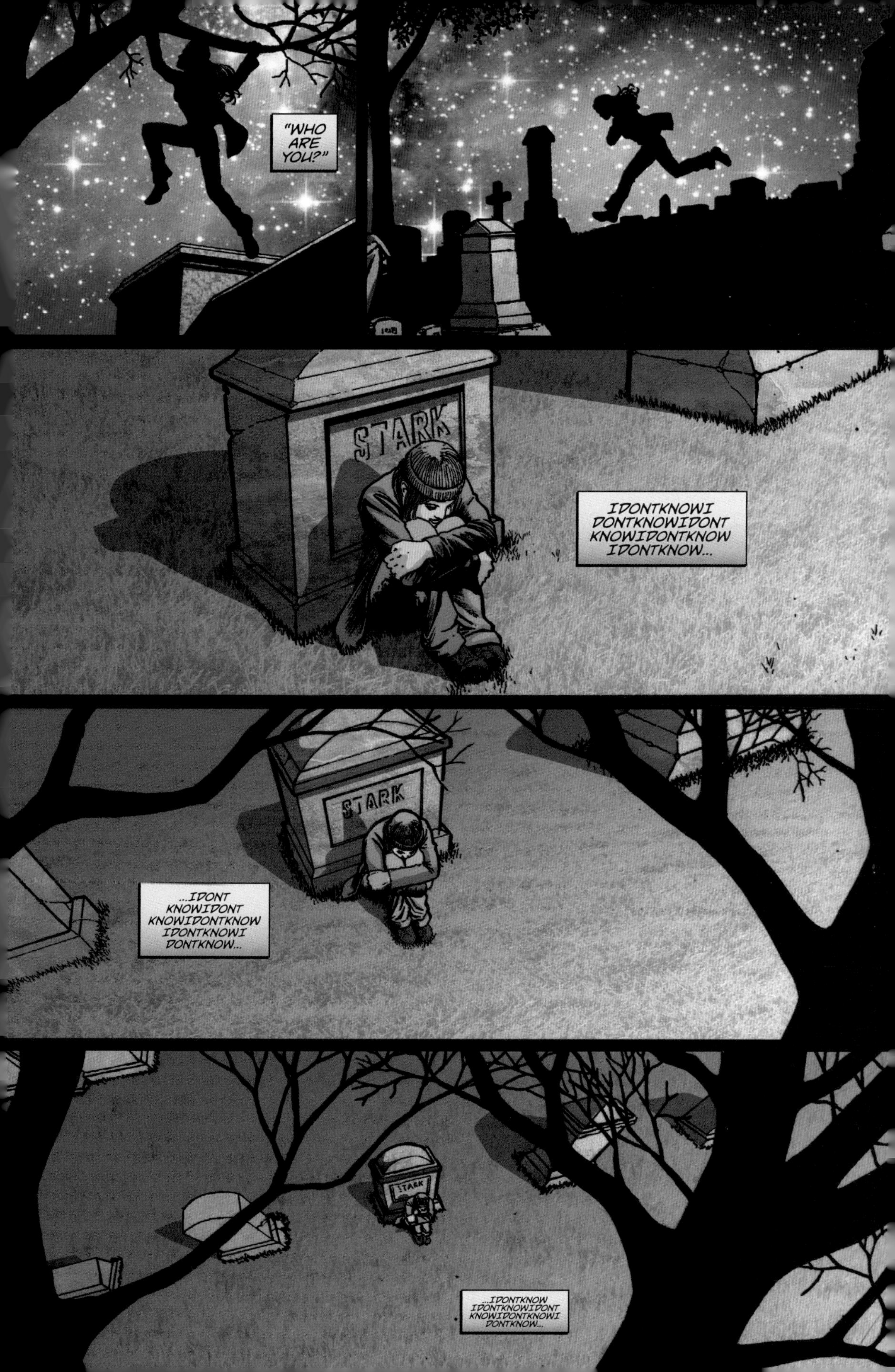
"WHO ARE YOU?"
STARK
IDONTKNOWI DONTKNOWIDONT KNOWIDONTKNOW IDONTKNOW...
STARK
...IDONT KNOWIDONT KNOWIDONTKNOW IDONTKNOWI DONTKNOW...
STARK
...IDONTKNOW IDONTKNOWIDONT KNOWIDONTKNOWI DONTKNOW...

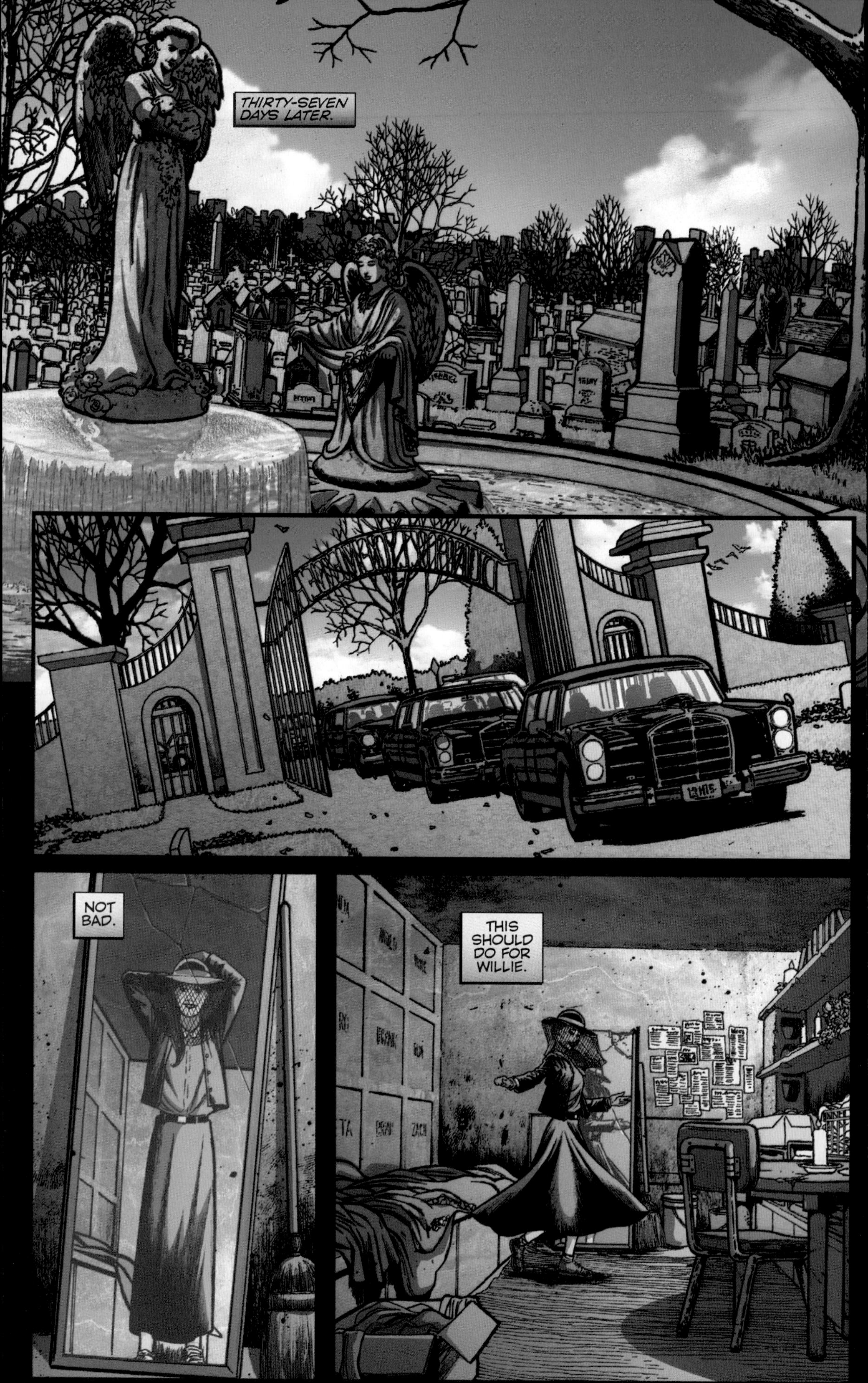
THIRTY-SEVEN DAYS LATER.
NOT BAD.
THIS SHOULD DO FOR WILLIE.

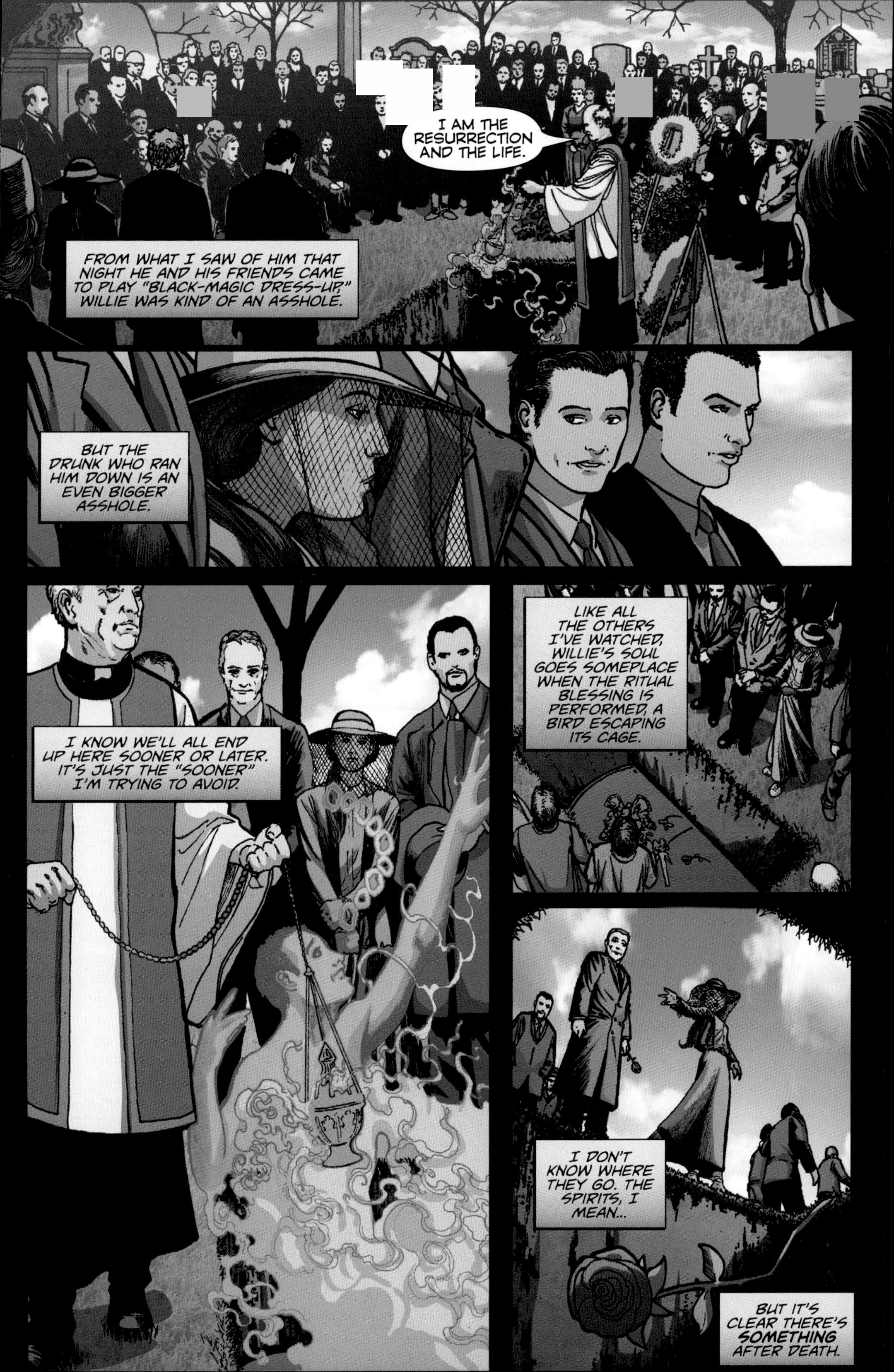
I AM THE RESURRECTION AND THE LIFE.
FROM WHAT I SAW OF HIM THAT NIGHT HE AND HIS FRIENDS CAME TO PLAY "BLACK-MAGIC DRESS-UP," WILLIE WAS KIND OF AN ASSHOLE.
BUT THE DRUNK WHO RAN HIM DOWN IS AN EVEN BIGGER ASSHOLE.
I KNOW WE'LL ALL END UP HERE SOONER OR LATER. IT'S JUST THE "SOONER" I'M TRYING TO AVOID.
LIKE ALL THE OTHERS I'VE WATCHED, WILLIE'S SOUL GOES SOMEPLACE WHEN THE RITUAL BLESSING IS PERFORMED, A BIRD ESCAPING ITS CAGE.
I DON'T KNOW WHERE THEY GO. THE SPIRITS, I MEAN...
BUT IT'S CLEAR THERE'S **SOMETHING** AFTER DEATH.

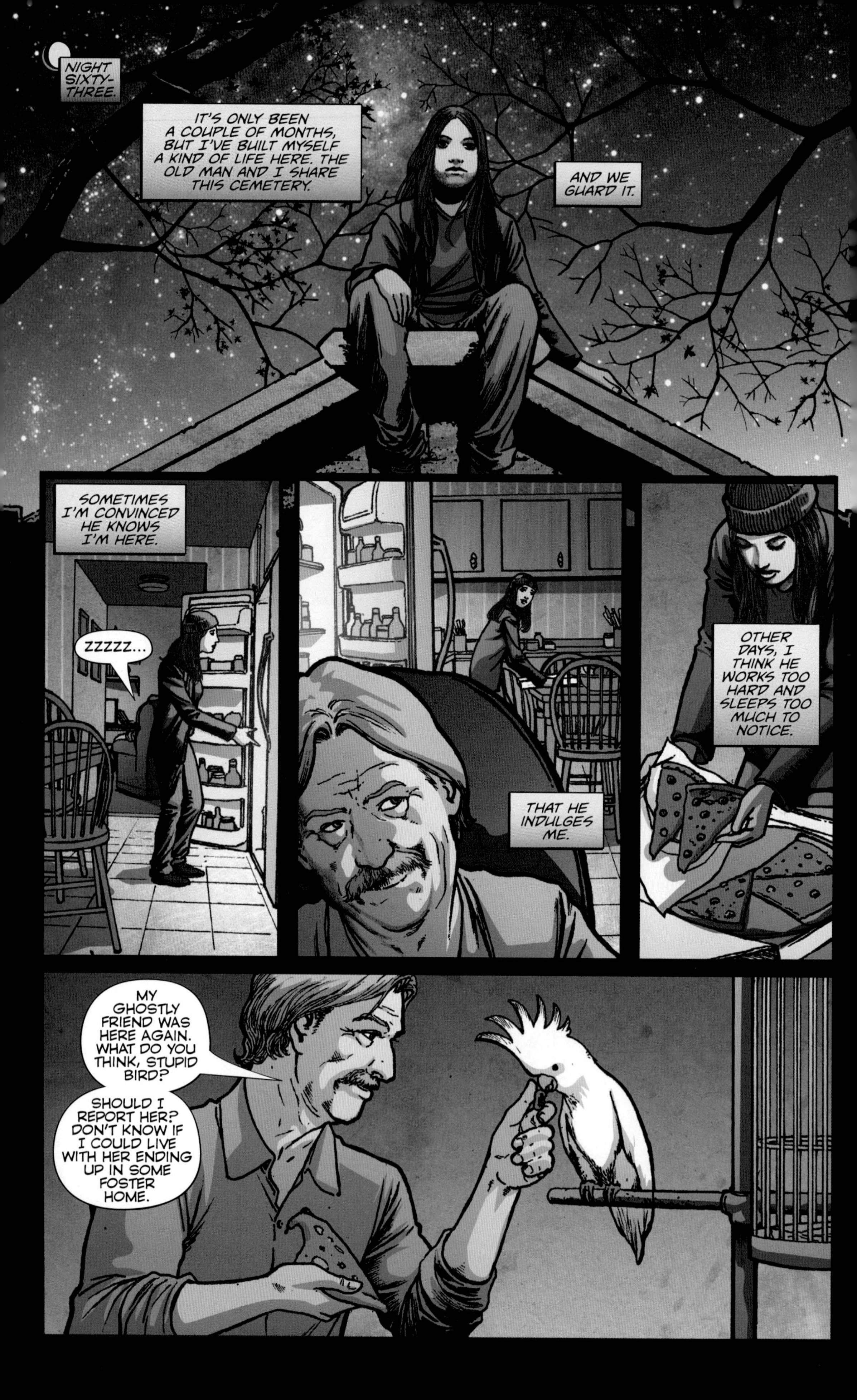
NIGHT SIXTY-THREE.
IT'S ONLY BEEN A COUPLE OF MONTHS, BUT I'VE BUILT MYSELF A KIND OF LIFE HERE. THE OLD MAN AND I SHARE THIS CEMETERY.
AND WE GUARD IT.
SOMETIMES I'M CONVINCED HE KNOWS I'M HERE.
ZZZZZ...
THAT HE INDULGES ME.
OTHER DAYS, I THINK HE WORKS TOO HARD AND SLEEPS TOO MUCH TO NOTICE.
MY GHOSTLY FRIEND WAS HERE AGAIN. WHAT DO YOU THINK, STUPID BIRD?
SHOULD I REPORT HER? DON'T KNOW IF I COULD LIVE WITH HER ENDING UP IN SOME FOSTER HOME.

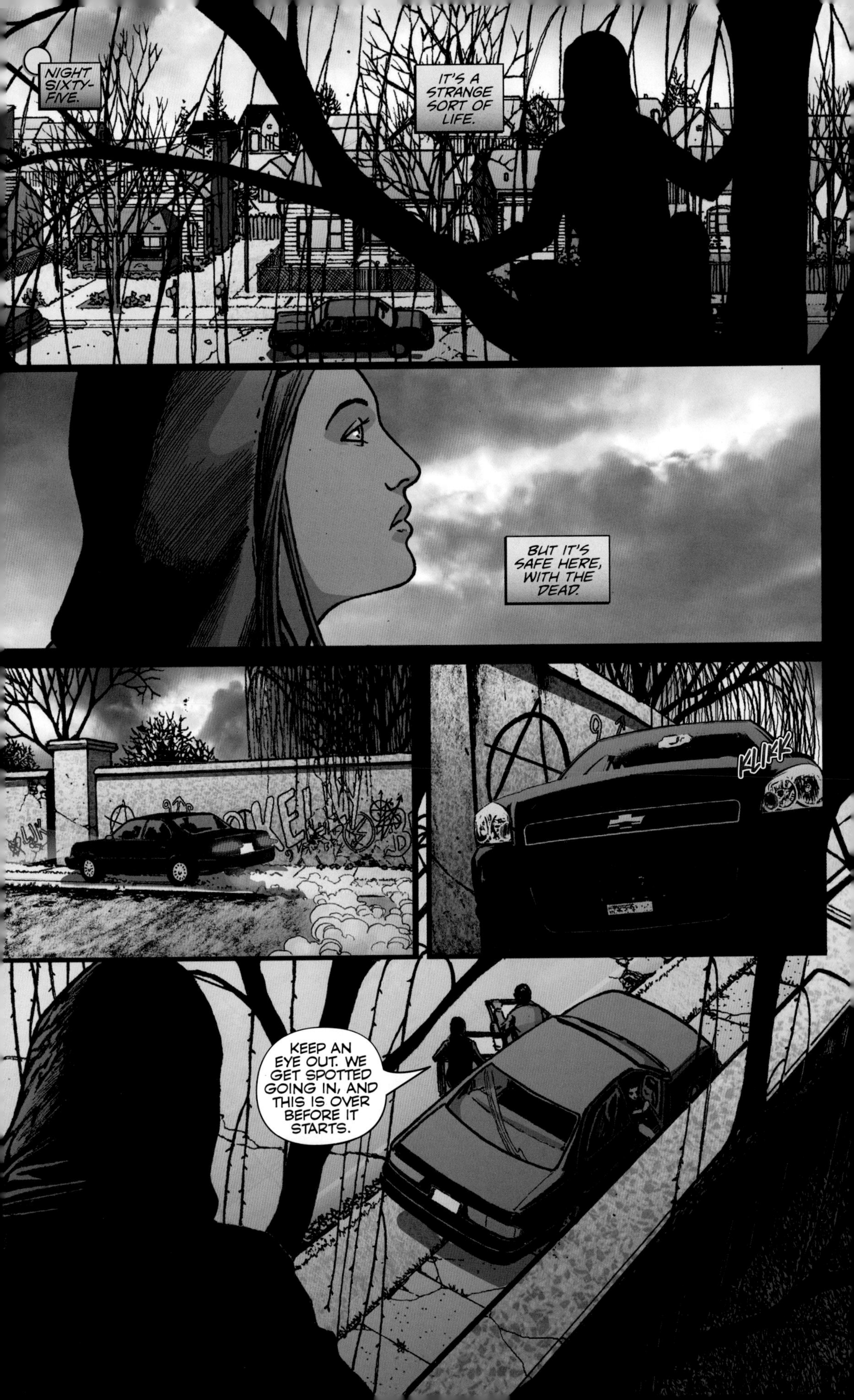
NIGHT SIXTY-FIVE.
IT'S A STRANGE SORT OF LIFE.
BUT IT'S SAFE HERE, WITH THE DEAD.
KLIKK
KEEP AN EYE OUT. WE GET SPOTTED GOING IN, AND THIS IS OVER BEFORE IT STARTS.

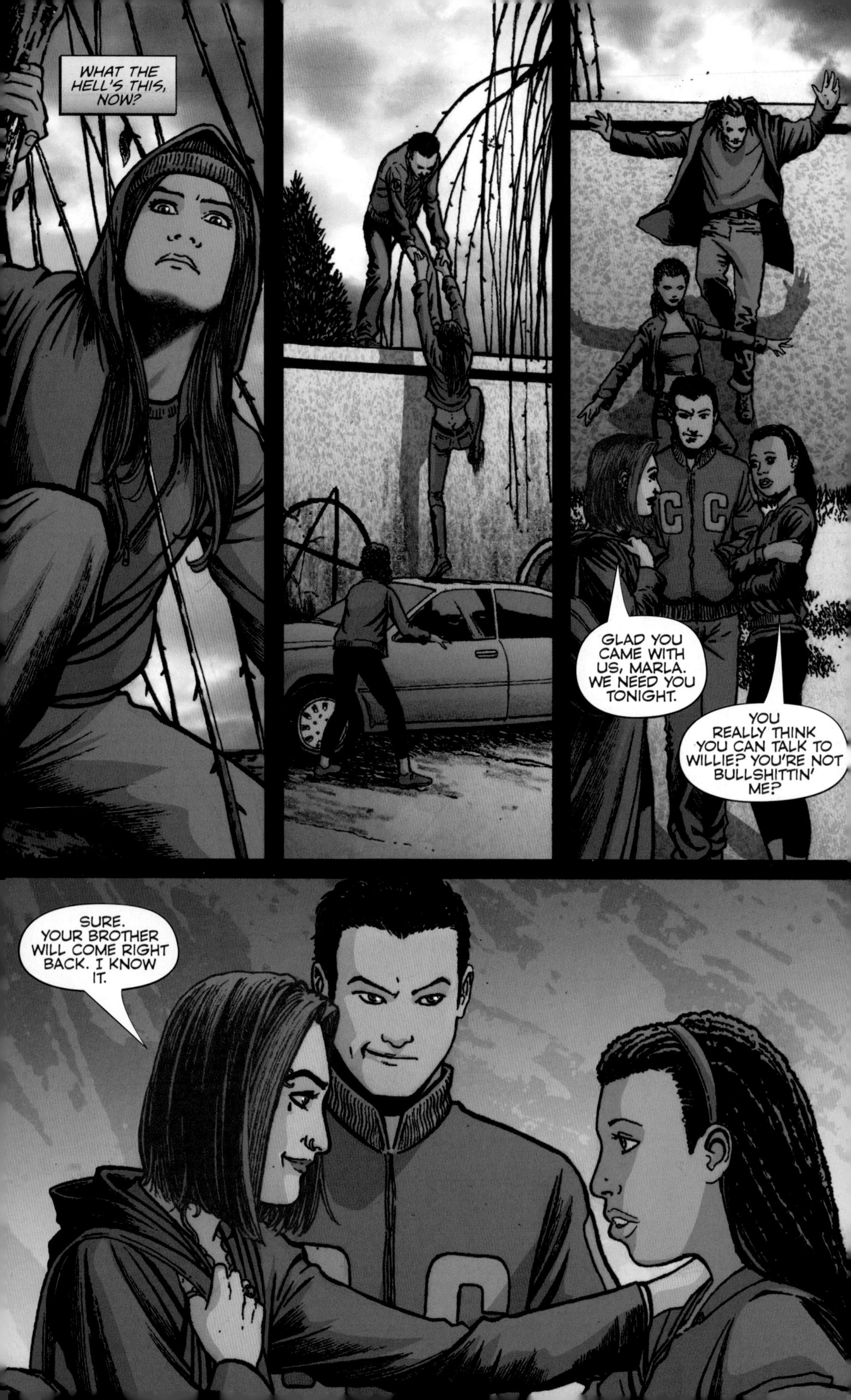
WHAT THE HELL'S THIS, NOW?
GLAD YOU CAME WITH US, MARLA. WE NEED YOU TONIGHT.
YOU REALLY THINK YOU CAN TALK TO WILLIE? YOU'RE NOT BULLSHITTIN' ME?
SURE. YOUR BROTHER WILL COME RIGHT BACK. I KNOW IT.

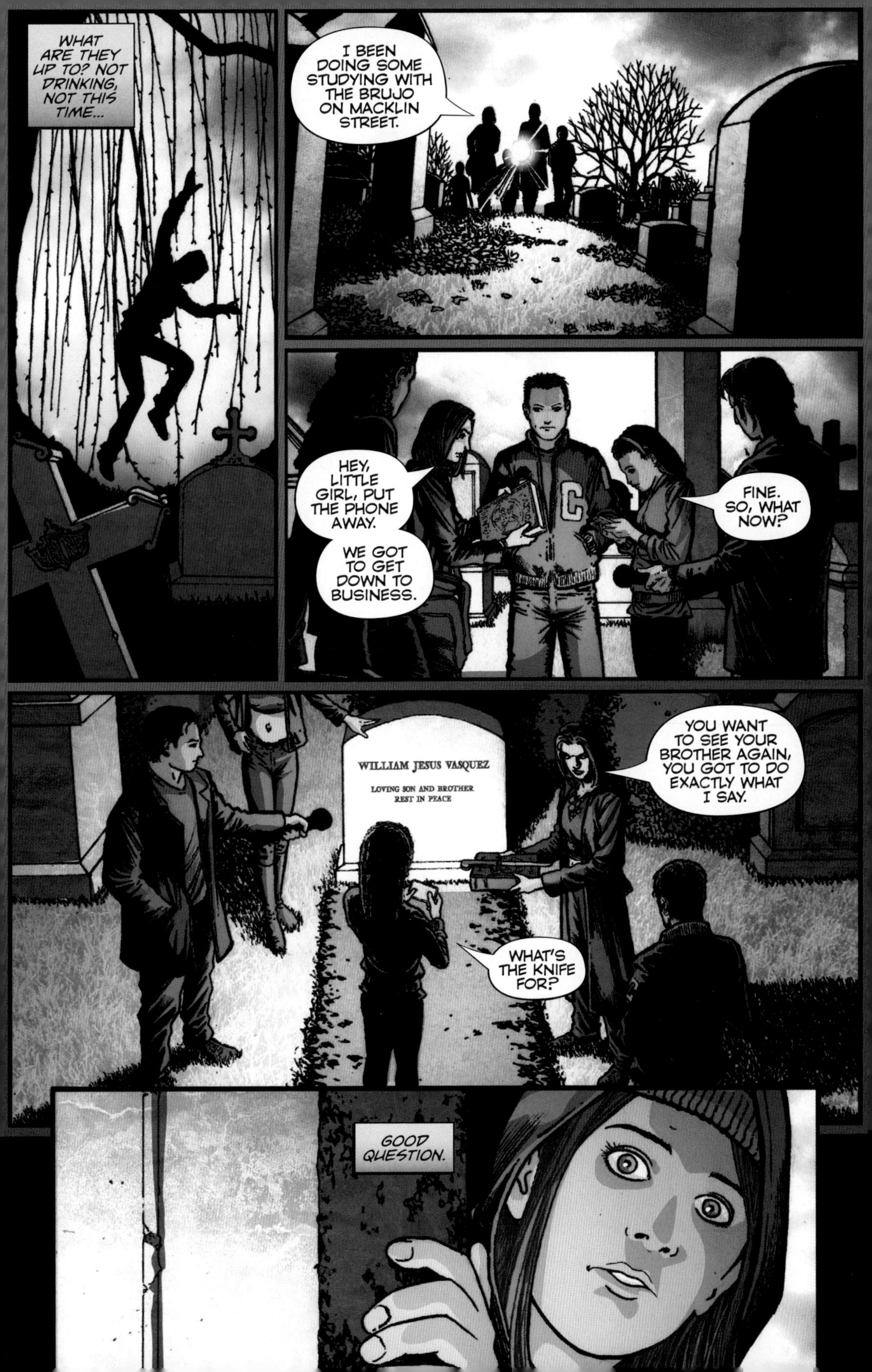
WHAT ARE THEY UP TO? NOT DRINKING, NOT THIS TIME...
I BEEN DOING SOME STUDYING WITH THE BRUJO ON MACKLIN STREET.
HEY, LITTLE GIRL, PUT THE PHONE AWAY.
WE GOT TO GET DOWN TO BUSINESS.
FINE. SO, WHAT NOW?
WILLIAM JESUS VASQUEZ
LOVING SON AND BROTHER
REST IN PEACE
YOU WANT TO SEE YOUR BROTHER AGAIN, YOU GOT TO DO EXACTLY WHAT I SAY.
WHAT'S THE KNIFE FOR?
GOOD QUESTION.

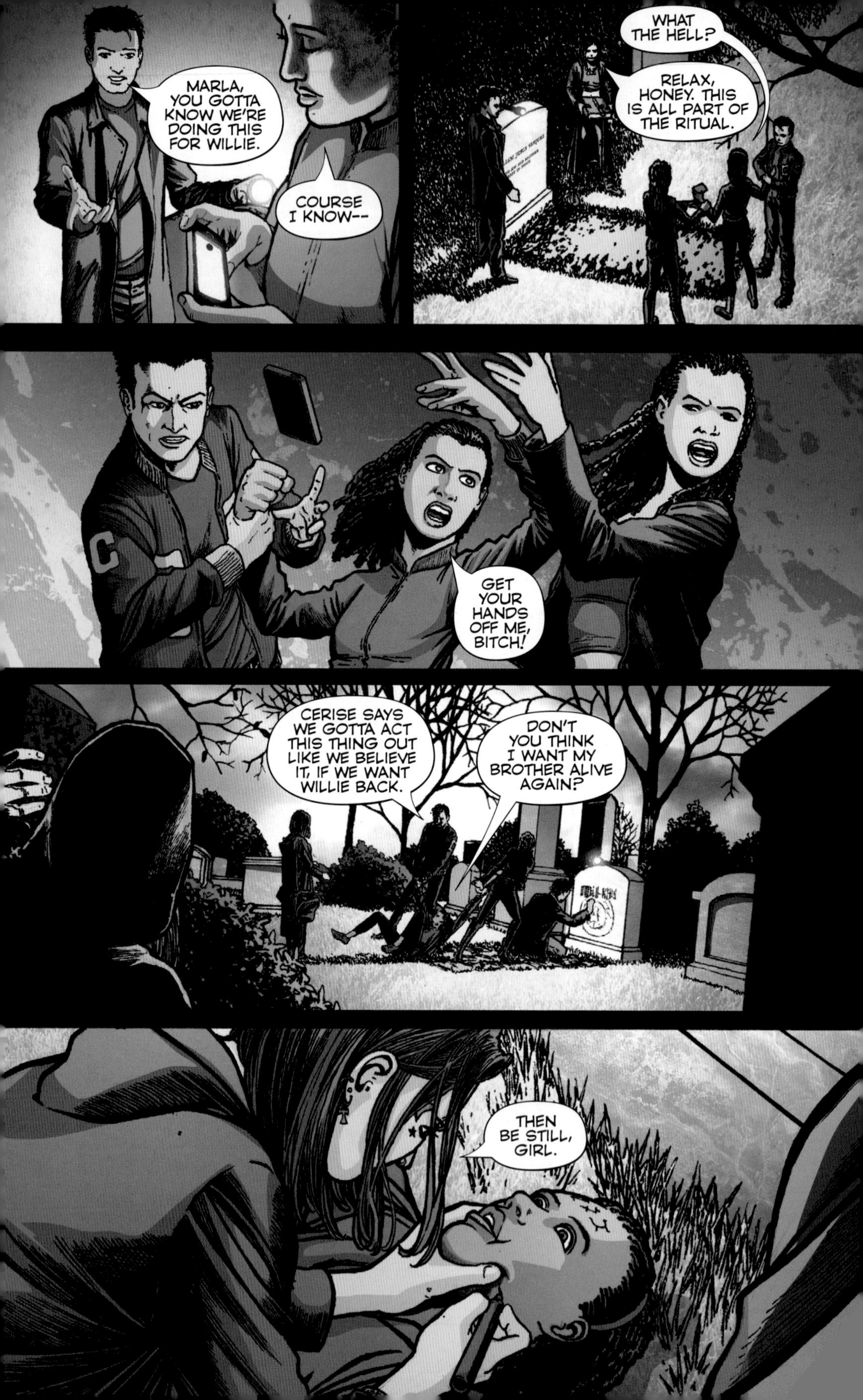
MARLA, YOU GOTTA KNOW WE'RE DOING THIS FOR WILLIE.
COURSE I KNOW--
WHAT THE HELL?
RELAX, HONEY. THIS IS ALL PART OF THE RITUAL.
GET YOUR HANDS OFF ME, BITCH!
CERISE SAYS WE GOTTA ACT THIS THING OUT LIKE WE BELIEVE IT, IF WE WANT WILLIE BACK.
DON'T YOU THINK I WANT MY BROTHER ALIVE AGAIN?
THEN BE STILL, GIRL.

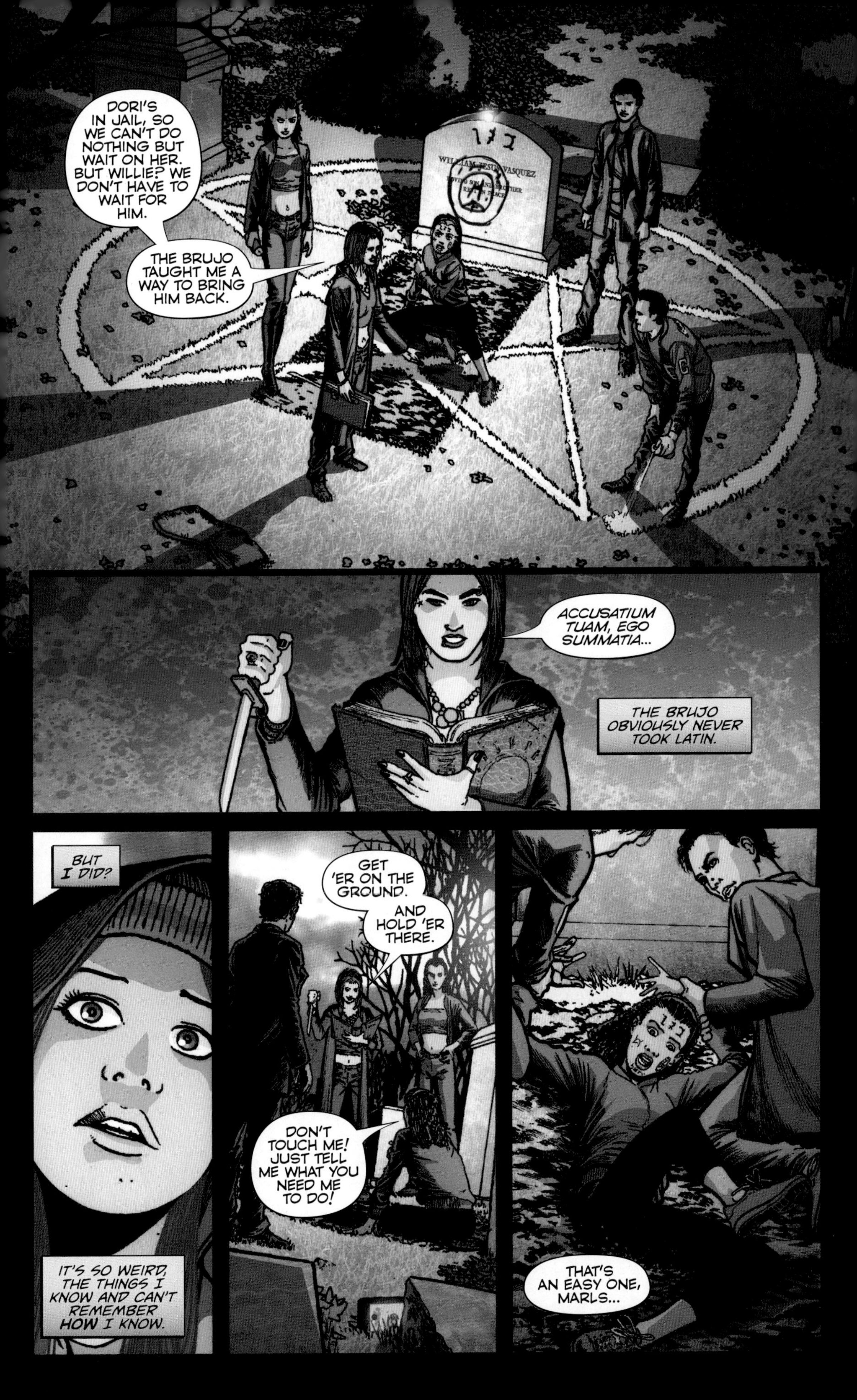
DORI'S IN JAIL, SO WE CAN'T DO NOTHING BUT WAIT ON HER. BUT WILLIE? WE DON'T HAVE TO WAIT FOR HIM.
THE BRUJO TAUGHT ME A WAY TO BRING HIM BACK.
ACCUSATIUM TUAM, EGO SUMMATIA...
THE BRUJO OBVIOUSLY NEVER TOOK LATIN.
BUT I DID?
IT'S SO WEIRD, THE THINGS I KNOW AND CAN'T REMEMBER HOW I KNOW.
GET 'ER ON THE GROUND.
AND HOLD 'ER THERE.
DON'T TOUCH ME! JUST TELL ME WHAT YOU NEED ME TO DO!
THAT'S AN EASY ONE, MARLS...

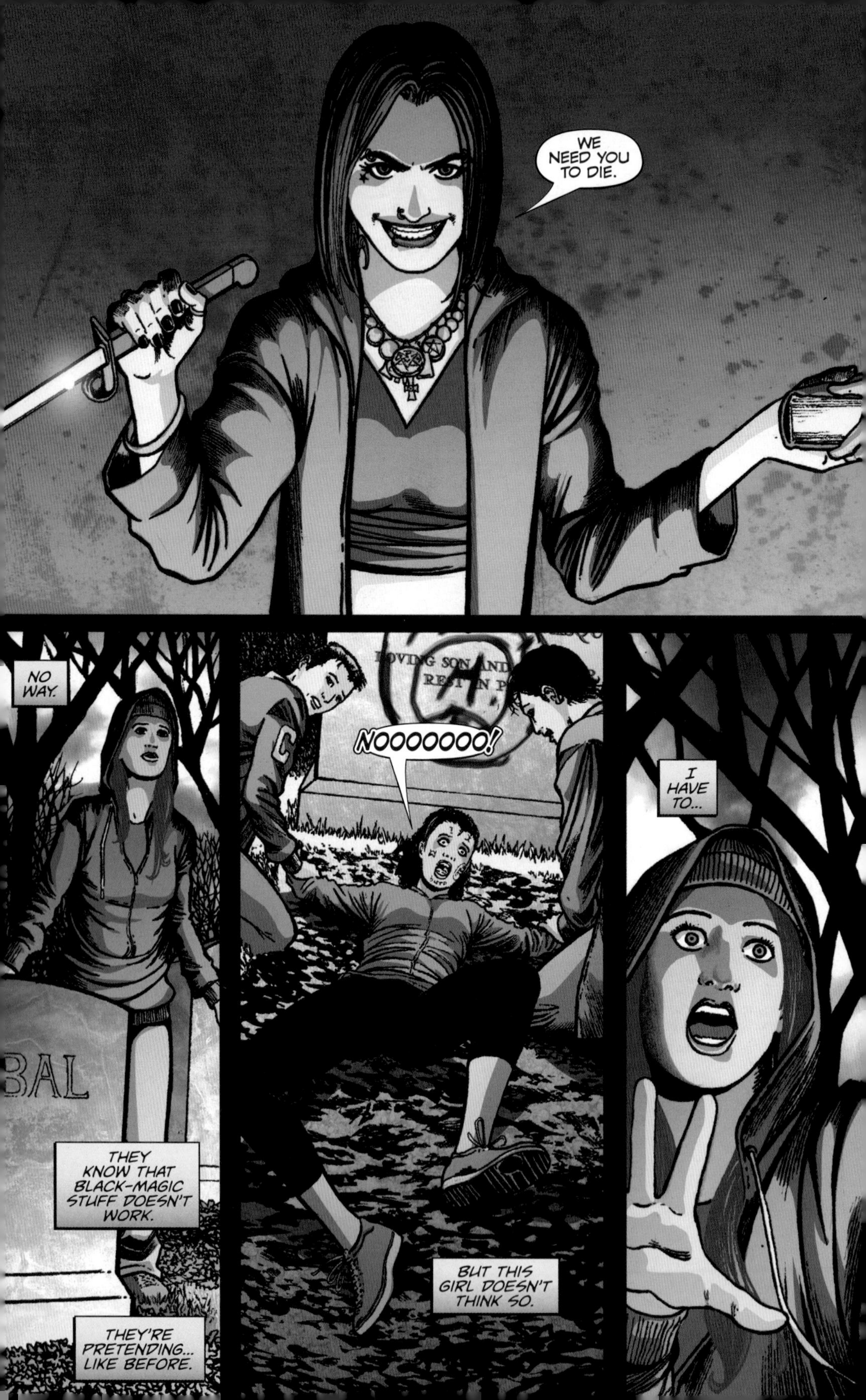
WE NEED YOU TO DIE.
NO WAY.
THEY KNOW THAT BLACK-MAGIC STUFF DOESN'T WORK.
THEY'RE PRETENDING... LIKE BEFORE.
NOOOOOOOO!
BUT THIS GIRL DOESN'T THINK SO.
I HAVE TO...

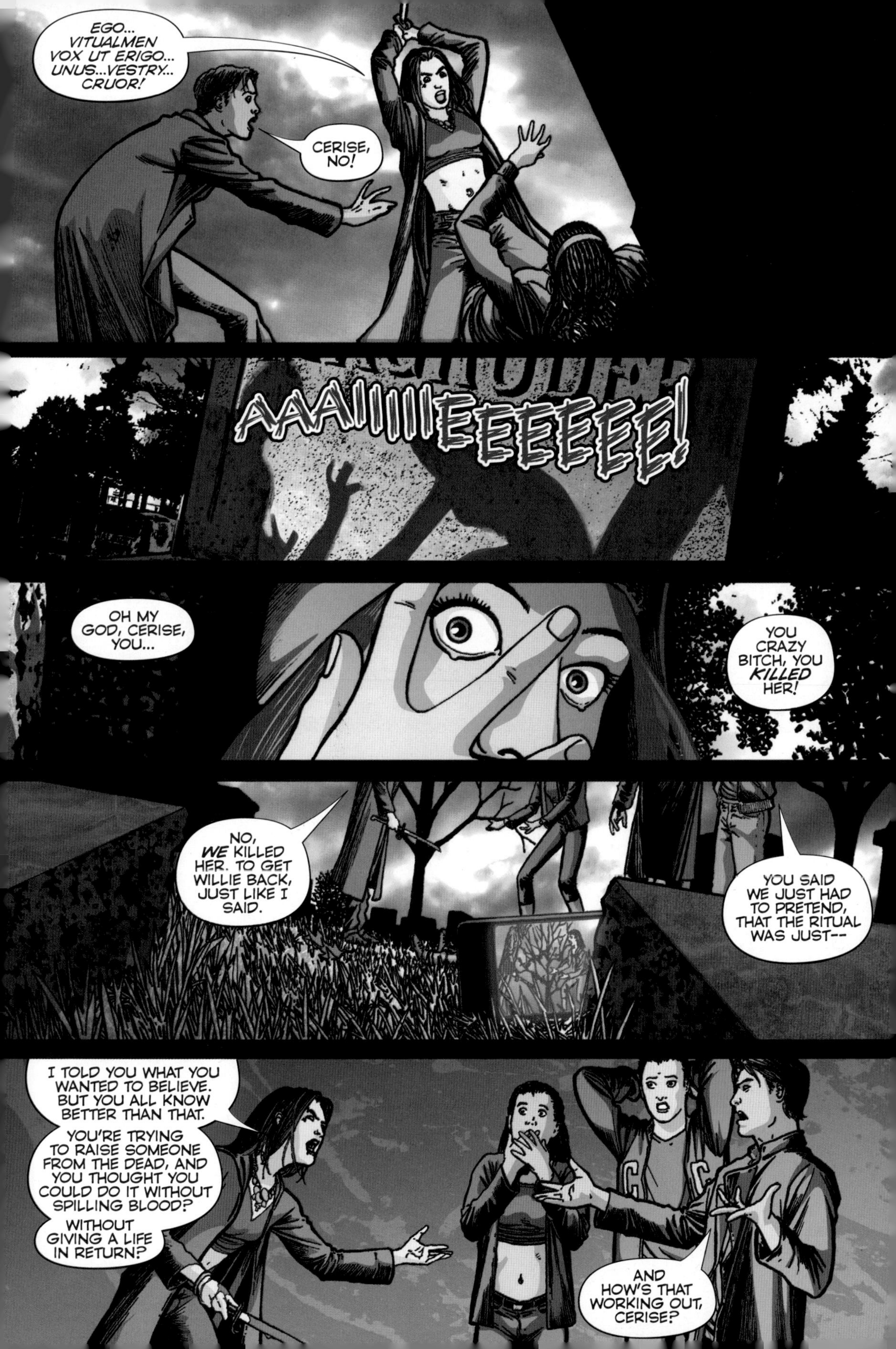
EGO... VITUALMEN VOX UT ERIGO... UNUS...VESTRY... CRUOR!
CERISE, NO!
AAAIIIIIIEEEEEEE!
OH MY GOD, CERISE, YOU...
YOU CRAZY BITCH, YOU KILLED HER!
NO, WE KILLED HER. TO GET WILLIE BACK, JUST LIKE I SAID.
YOU SAID WE JUST HAD TO PRETEND, THAT THE RITUAL WAS JUST--
I TOLD YOU WHAT YOU WANTED TO BELIEVE. BUT YOU ALL KNOW BETTER THAN THAT.
YOU'RE TRYING TO RAISE SOMEONE FROM THE DEAD, AND YOU THOUGHT YOU COULD DO IT WITHOUT SPILLING BLOOD?
WITHOUT GIVING A LIFE IN RETURN?
AND HOW'S THAT WORKING OUT, CERISE?

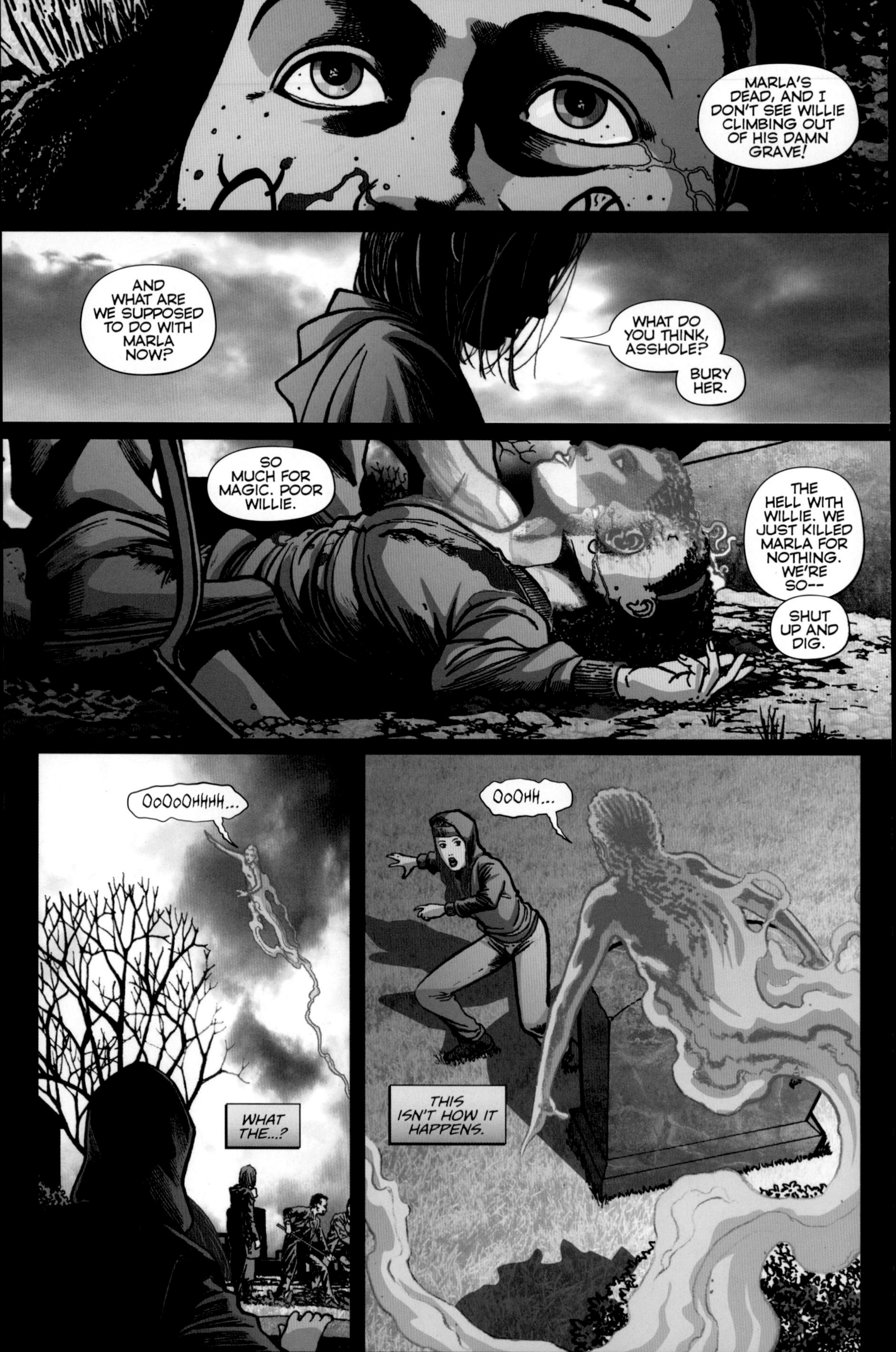
MARLA'S DEAD, AND I DON'T SEE WILLIE CLIMBING OUT OF HIS DAMN GRAVE!
AND WHAT ARE WE SUPPOSED TO DO WITH MARLA NOW?
WHAT DO YOU THINK, ASSHOLE?
BURY HER.
SO MUCH FOR MAGIC. POOR WILLIE.
THE HELL WITH WILLIE. WE JUST KILLED MARLA FOR NOTHING. WE'RE SO--
SHUT UP AND DIG.
OOOOOHHHH...
WHAT THE...?
OOOHH...
THIS ISN'T HOW IT HAPPENS.

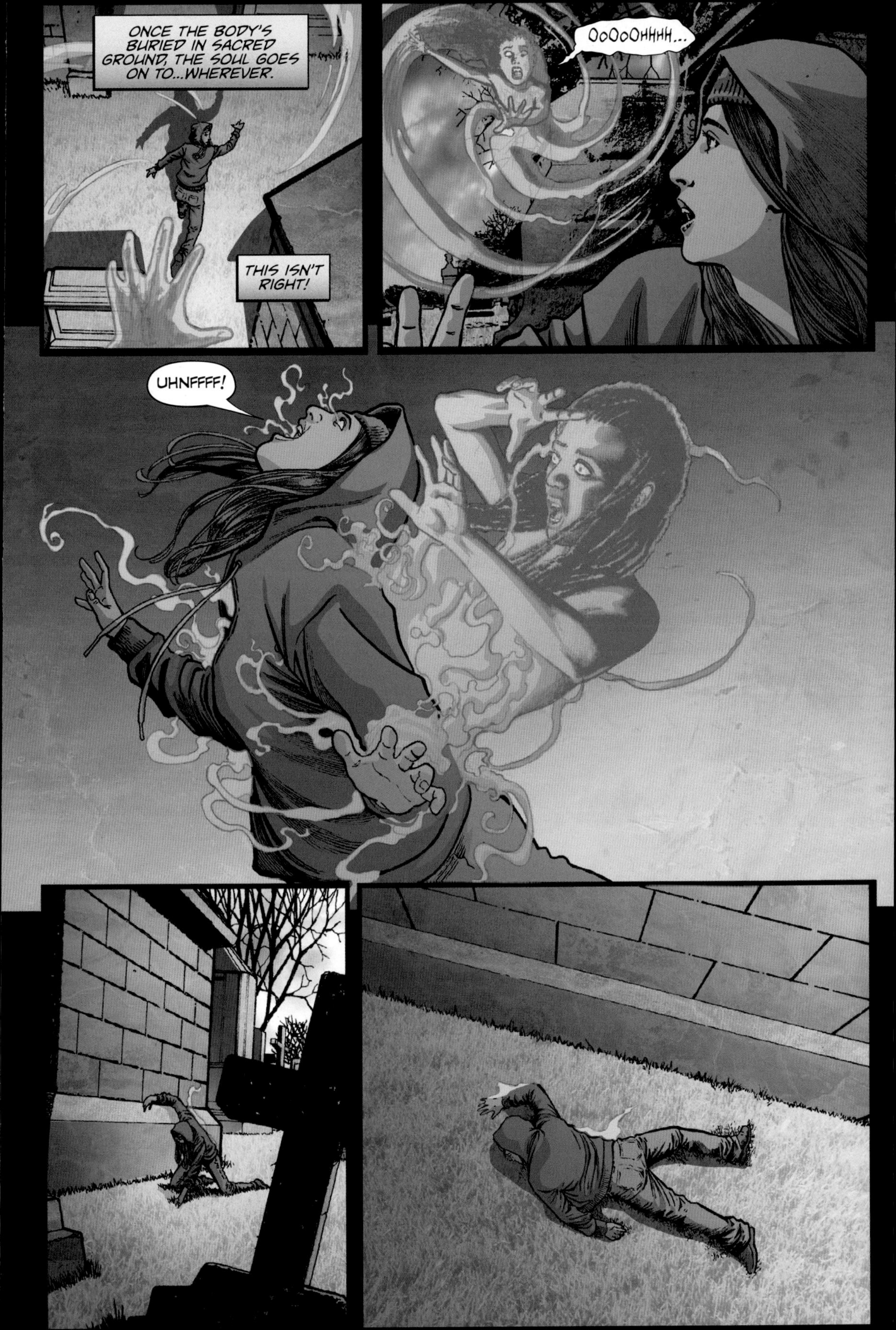
ONCE THE BODY'S BURIED IN SACRED GROUND, THE SOUL GOES ON TO...WHEREVER.
THIS ISN'T RIGHT!
OOOOOHHHH...
UHNFFFF!

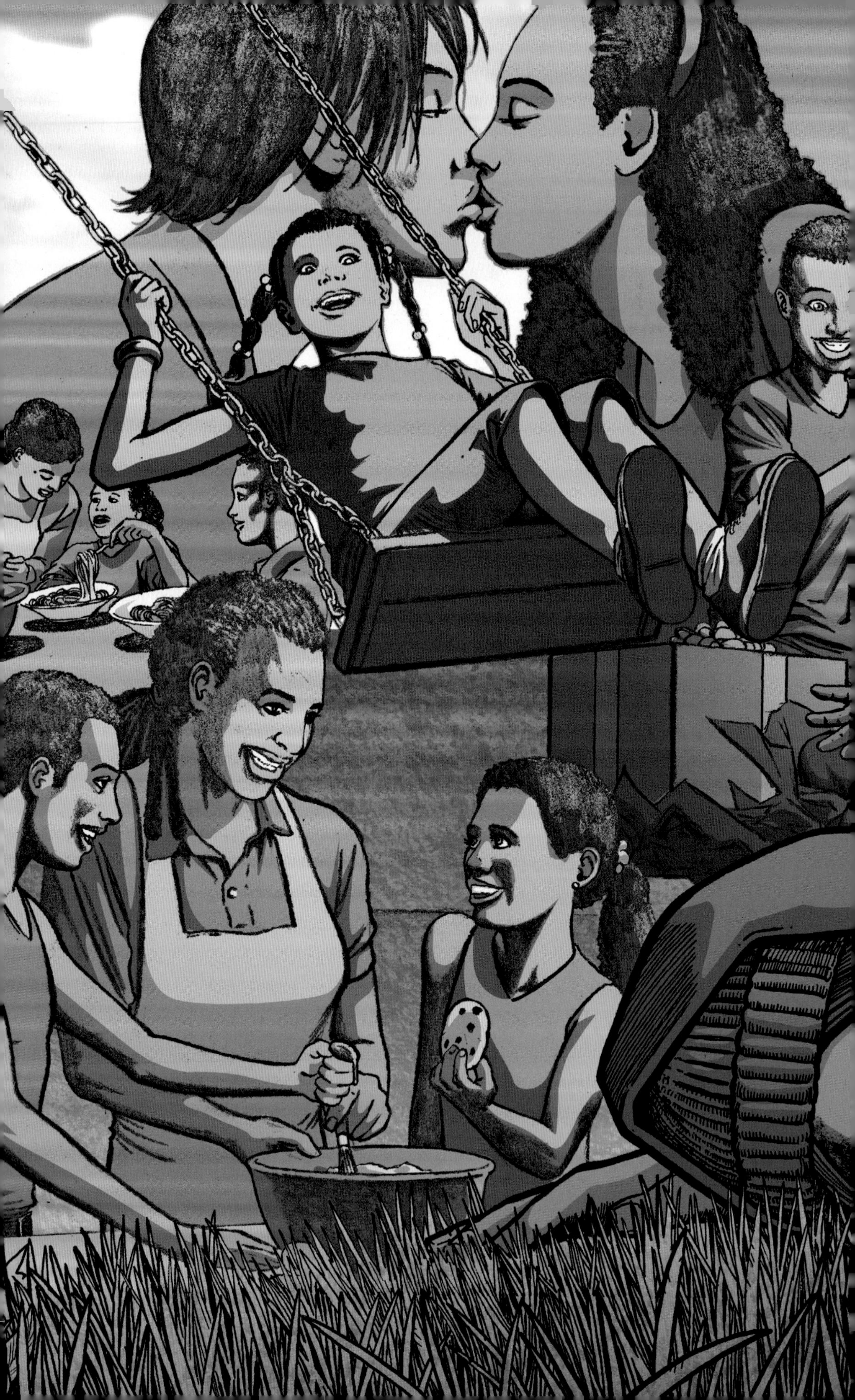

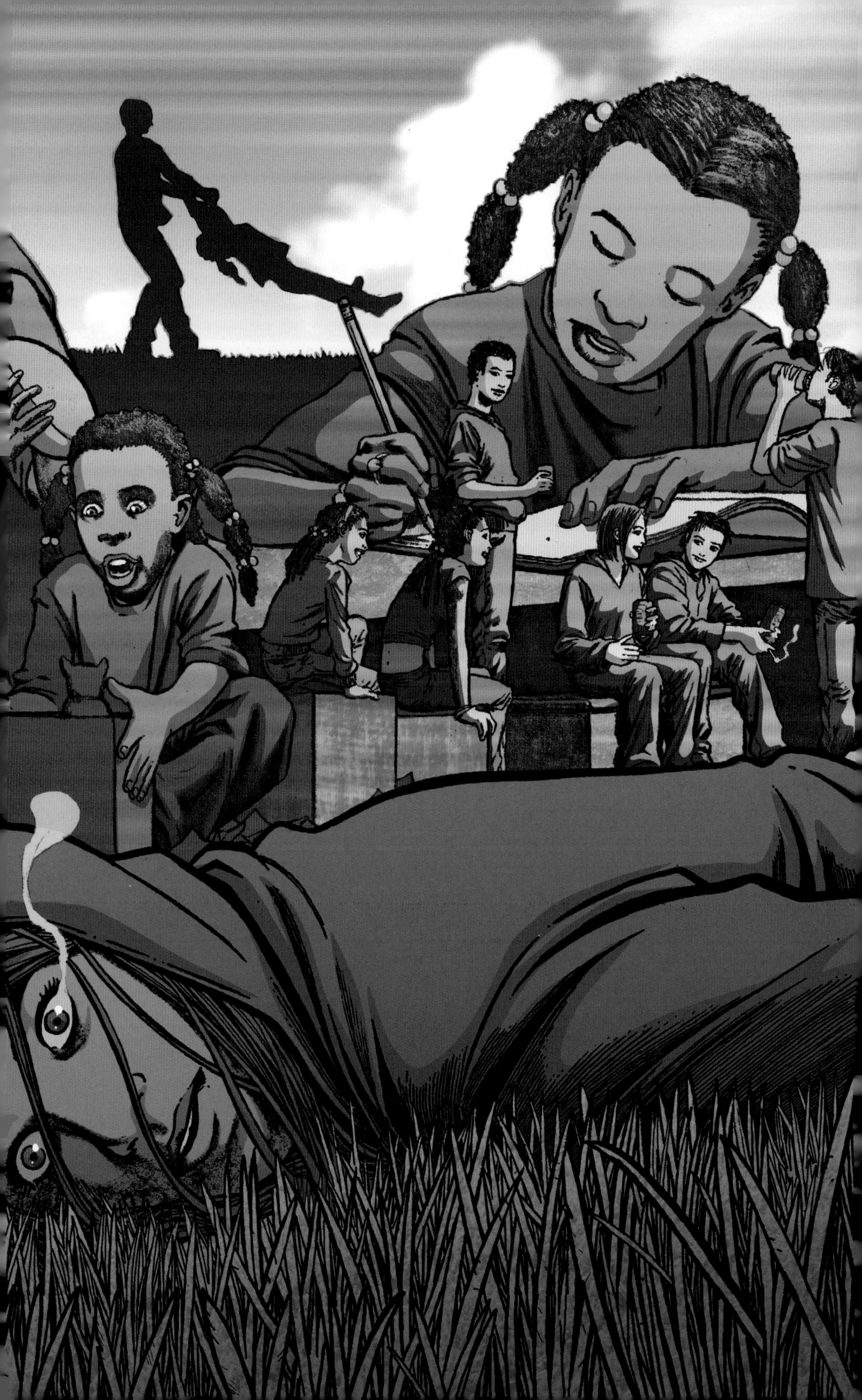

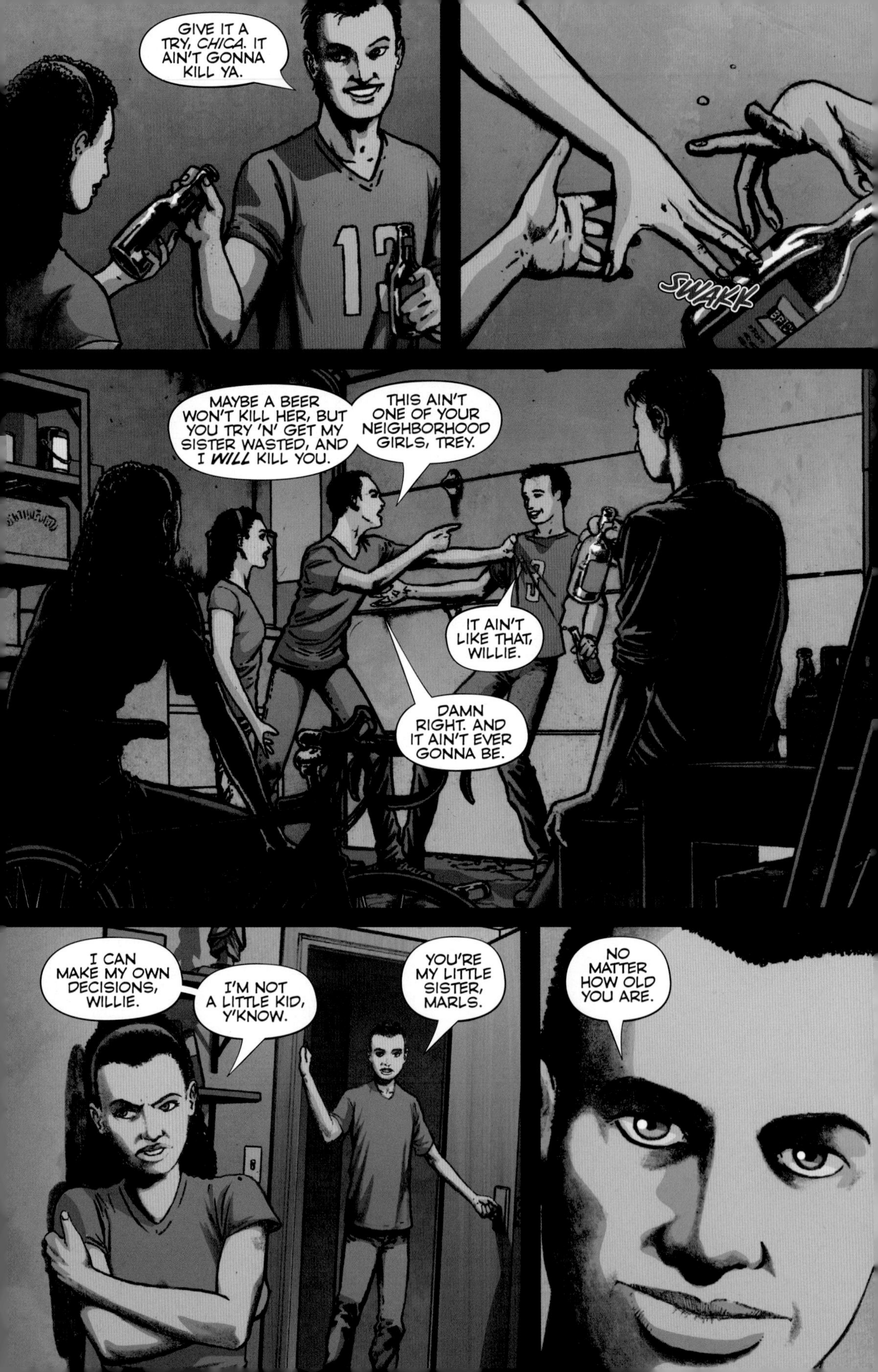
GIVE IT A TRY, CHICA. IT AIN'T GONNA KILL YA.
SWAKK
MAYBE A BEER WON'T KILL HER, BUT YOU TRY 'N' GET MY SISTER WASTED, AND I WILL KILL YOU.
THIS AIN'T ONE OF YOUR NEIGHBORHOOD GIRLS, TREY.
IT AIN'T LIKE THAT, WILLIE.
DAMN RIGHT. AND IT AIN'T EVER GONNA BE.
I CAN MAKE MY OWN DECISIONS, WILLIE.
I'M NOT A LITTLE KID, Y'KNOW.
YOU'RE MY LITTLE SISTER, MARLS.
NO MATTER HOW OLD YOU ARE.

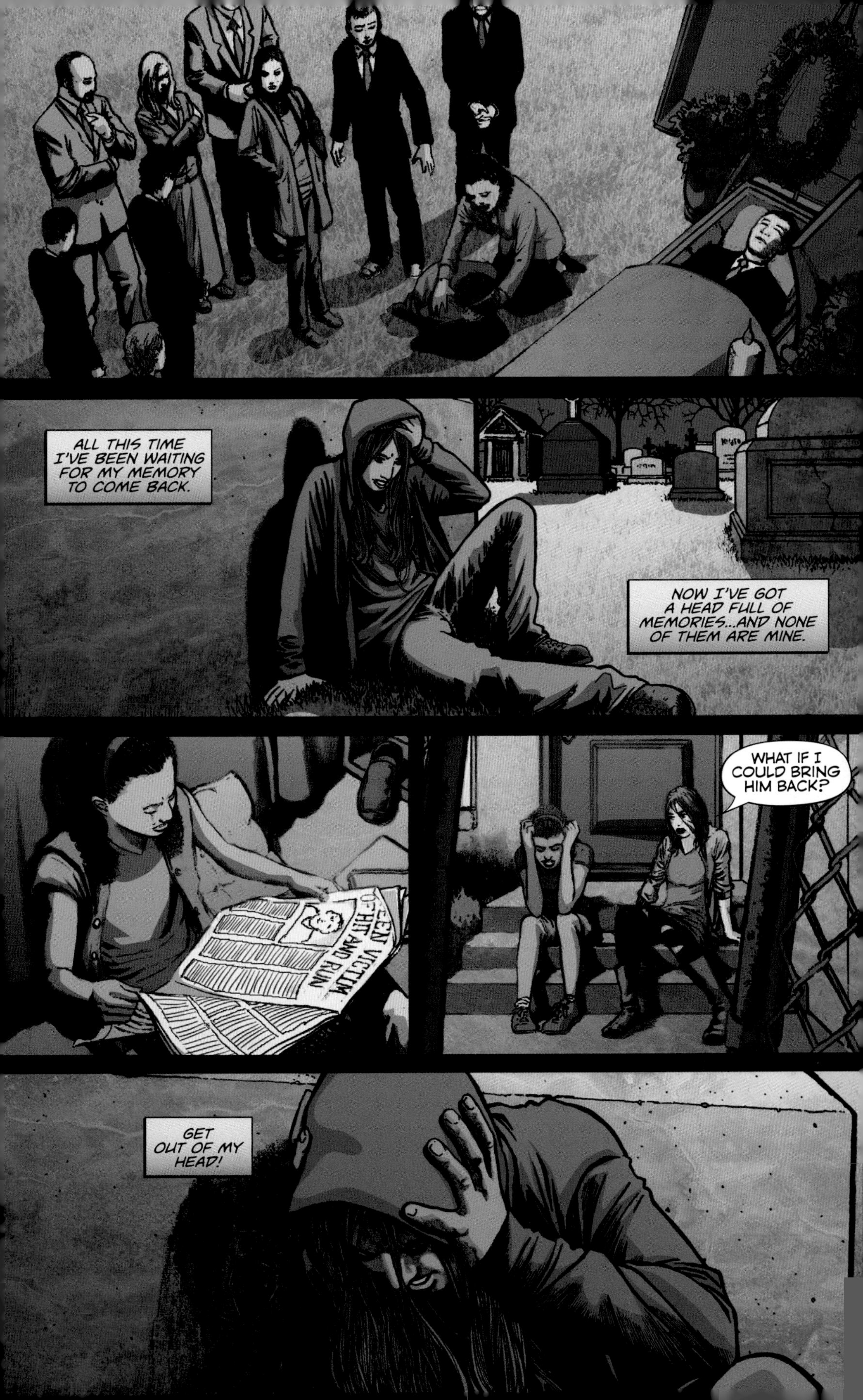
ALL THIS TIME I'VE BEEN WAITING FOR MY MEMORY TO COME BACK.
NOW I'VE GOT A HEAD FULL OF MEMORIES...AND NONE OF THEM ARE MINE.
EEN VICTIM
OF HIT AND RUN
WHAT IF I COULD BRING HIM BACK?
GET OUT OF MY HEAD!

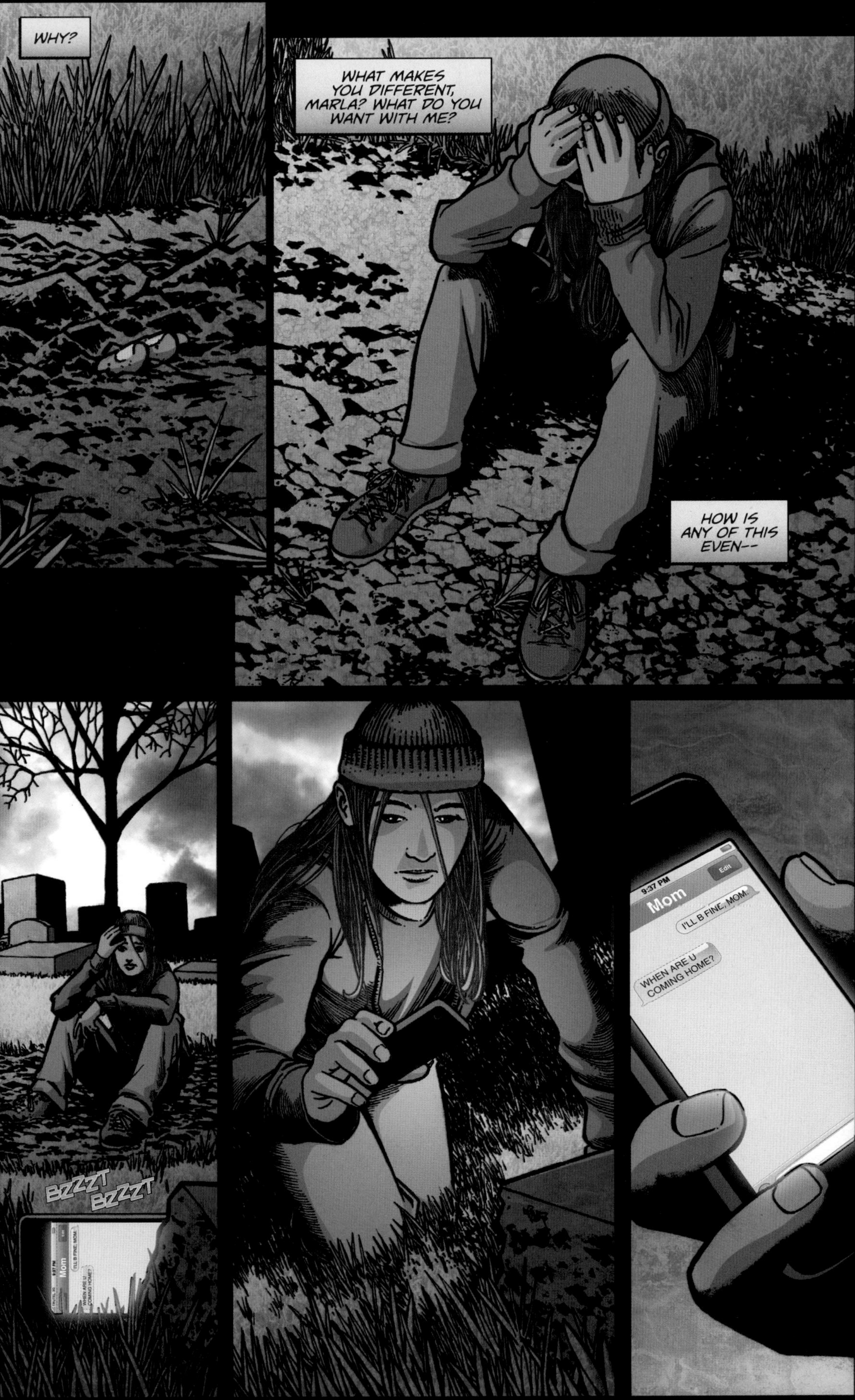
WHY?
WHAT MAKES YOU DIFFERENT, MARLA? WHAT DO YOU WANT WITH ME?
HOW IS ANY OF THIS EVEN--
BZZZT BZZZT
9:37 PM
Edit
Mom
I'LL B FINE, MOM.
WHEN ARE U COMING HOME?

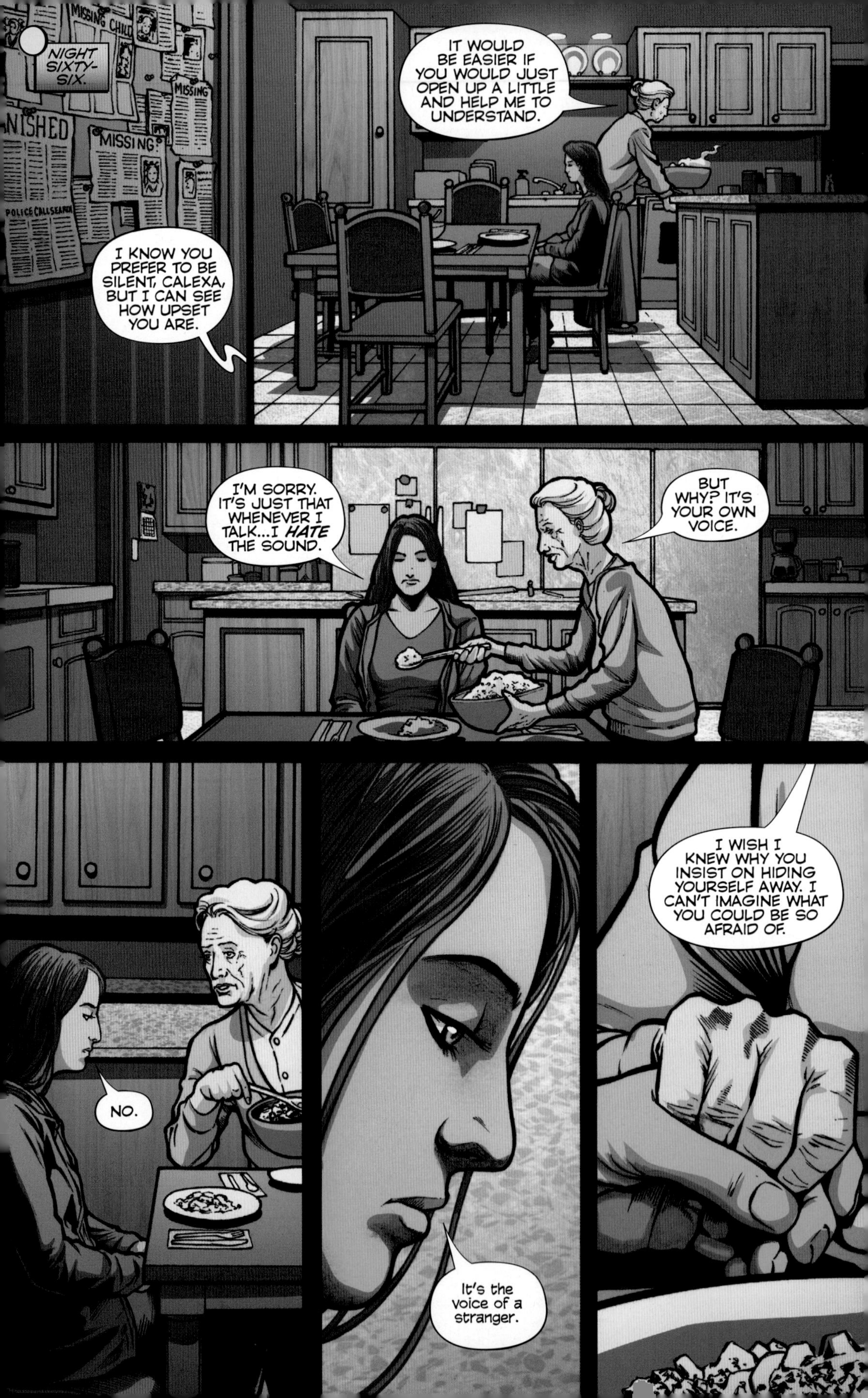
NIGHT SIXTY-SIX.
MISSING CHILD
MISSING
MISSING
NISHED
POLICE CALL SEARCH
I KNOW YOU PREFER TO BE SILENT, CALEXA, BUT I CAN SEE HOW UPSET YOU ARE.
IT WOULD BE EASIER IF YOU WOULD JUST OPEN UP A LITTLE AND HELP ME TO UNDERSTAND.
I'M SORRY. IT'S JUST THAT WHENEVER I TALK...I *HATE* THE SOUND.
BUT WHY? IT'S YOUR OWN VOICE.
NO.
It's the voice of a stranger.
I WISH I KNEW WHY YOU INSIST ON HIDING YOURSELF AWAY. I CAN'T IMAGINE WHAT YOU COULD BE SO AFRAID OF.

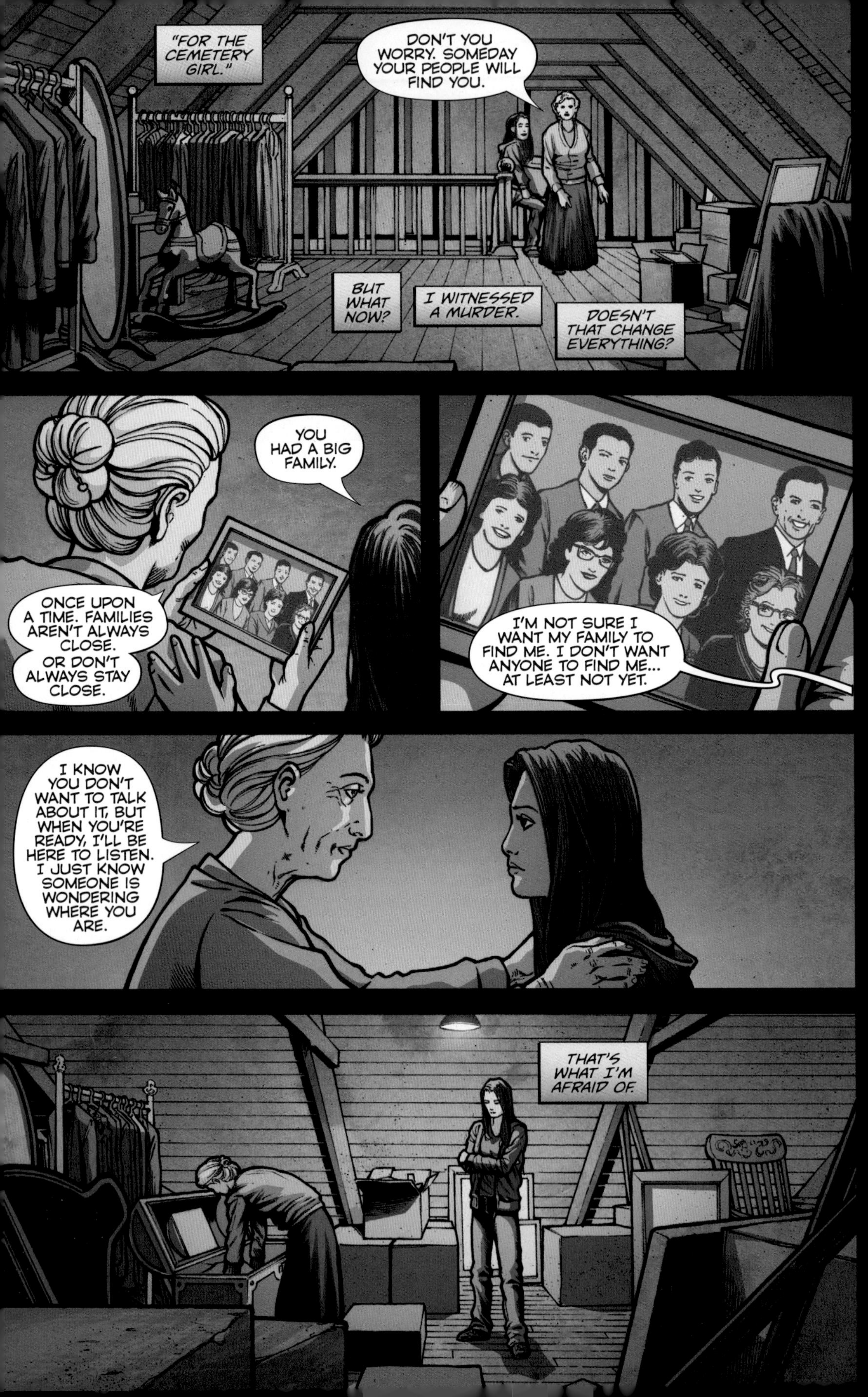
"FOR THE CEMETERY GIRL."
DON'T YOU WORRY. SOMEDAY YOUR PEOPLE WILL FIND YOU.
BUT WHAT NOW?
I WITNESSED A MURDER.
DOESN'T THAT CHANGE EVERYTHING?
YOU HAD A BIG FAMILY.
ONCE UPON A TIME. FAMILIES AREN'T ALWAYS CLOSE.
OR DON'T ALWAYS STAY CLOSE.
I'M NOT SURE I WANT MY FAMILY TO FIND ME. I DON'T WANT ANYONE TO FIND ME... AT LEAST NOT YET.
I KNOW YOU DON'T WANT TO TALK ABOUT IT, BUT WHEN YOU'RE READY, I'LL BE HERE TO LISTEN. I JUST KNOW SOMEONE IS WONDERING WHERE YOU ARE.
THAT'S WHAT I'M AFRAID OF.

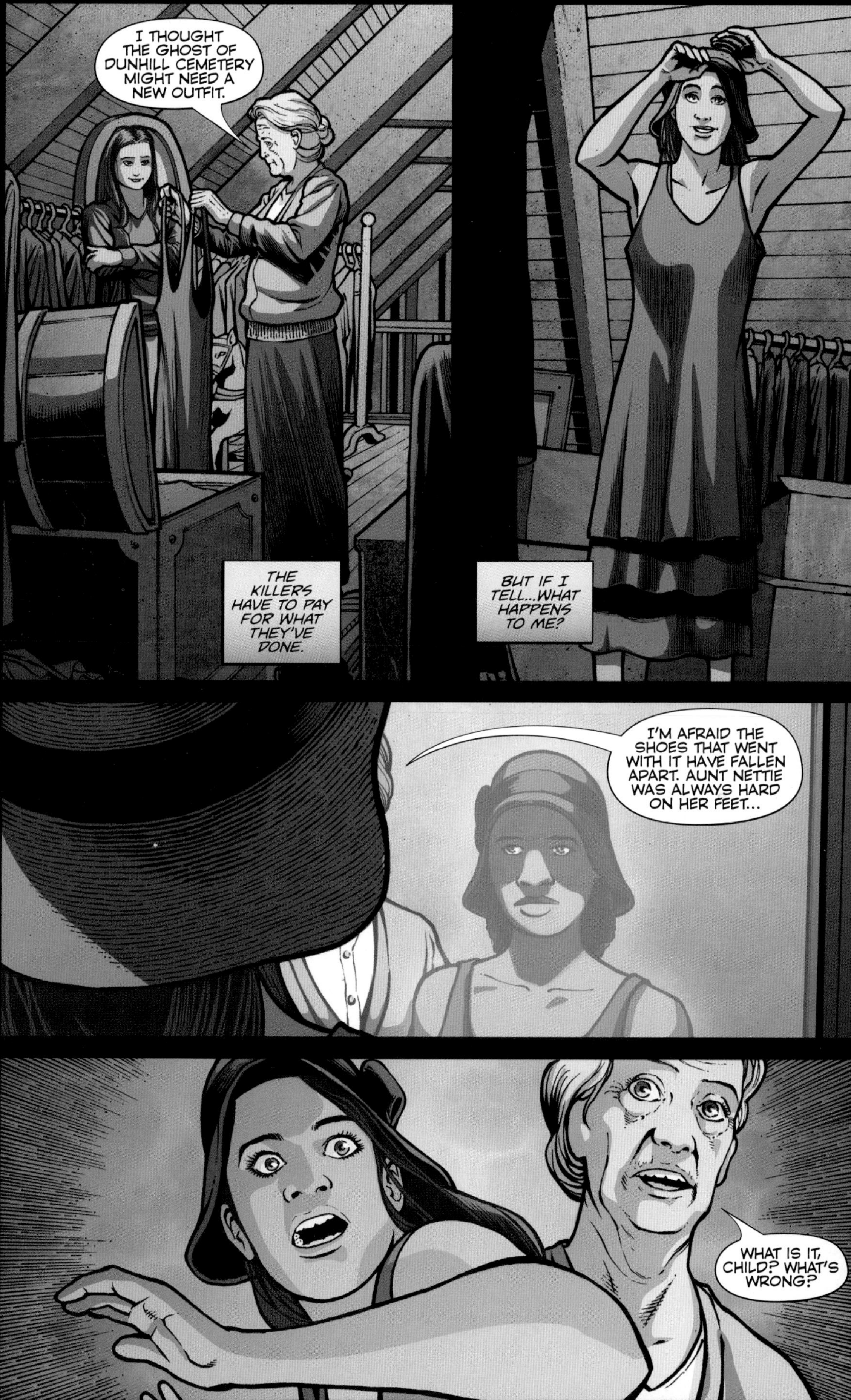
I THOUGHT THE GHOST OF DUNHILL CEMETERY MIGHT NEED A NEW OUTFIT.
THE KILLERS HAVE TO PAY FOR WHAT THEY'VE DONE.
BUT IF I TELL...WHAT HAPPENS TO ME?
I'M AFRAID THE SHOES THAT WENT WITH IT HAVE FALLEN APART. AUNT NETTIE WAS ALWAYS HARD ON HER FEET...
WHAT IS IT, CHILD? WHAT'S WRONG?

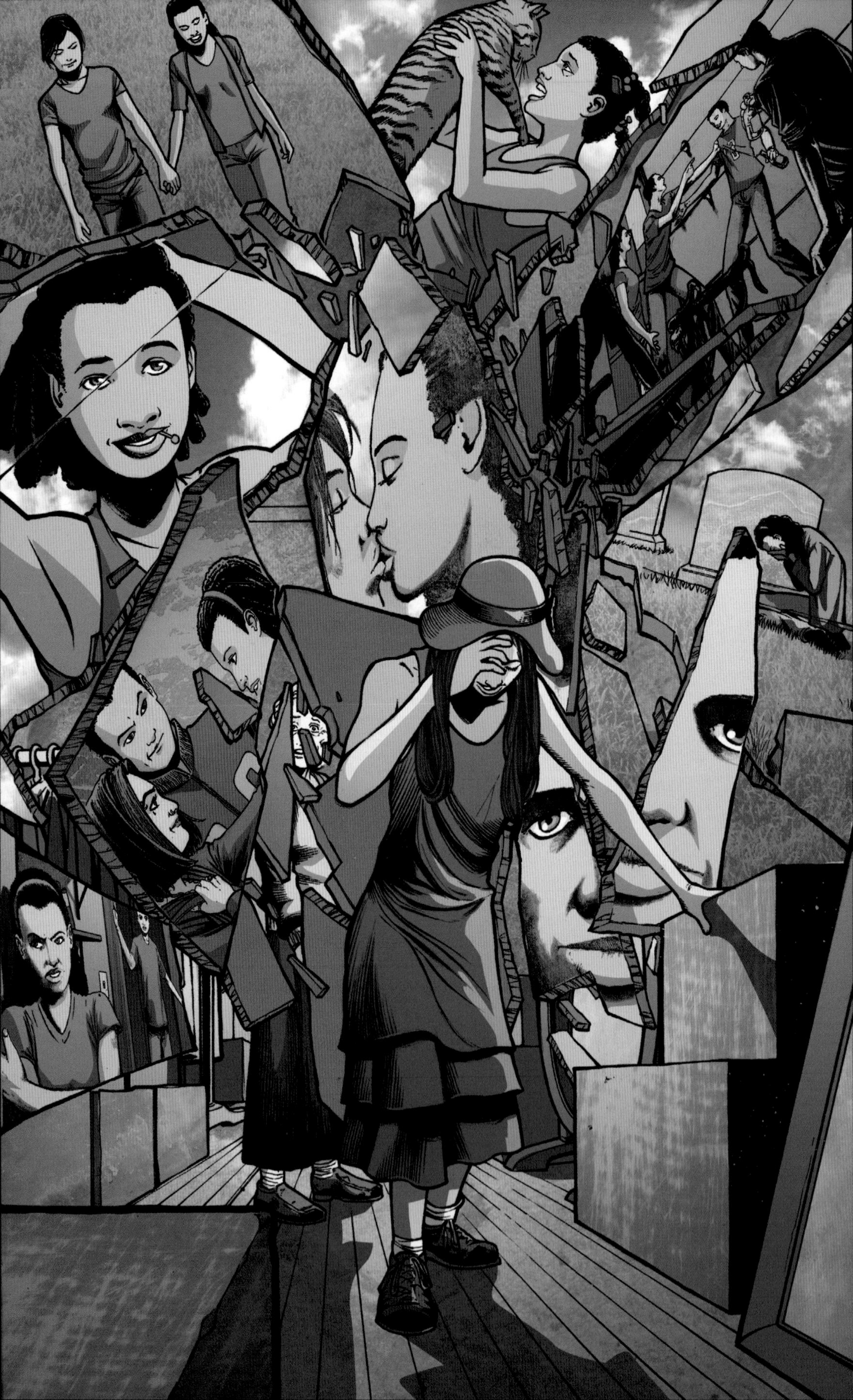

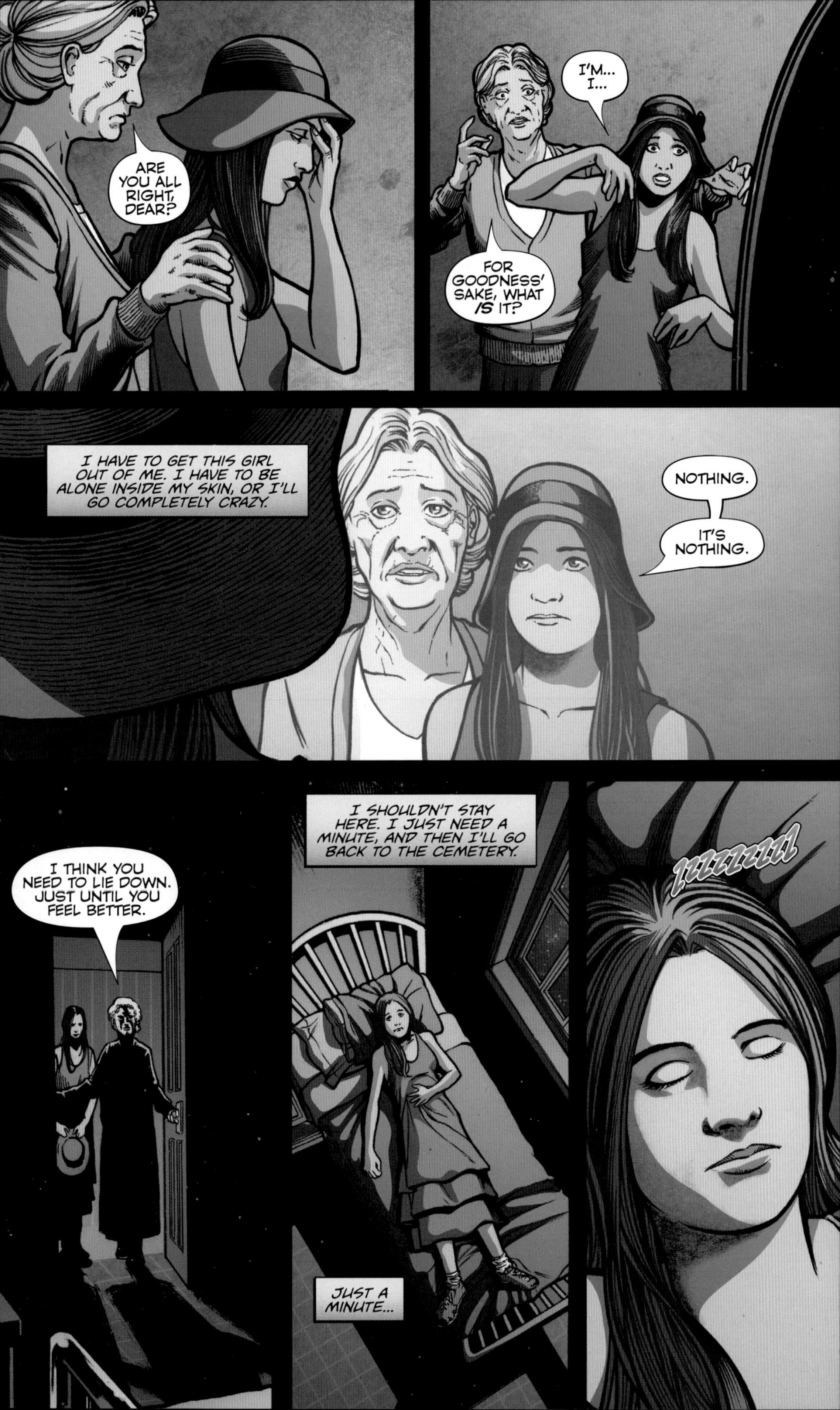

ARE YOU ALL RIGHT, DEAR?
I'M... I...
FOR GOODNESS' SAKE, WHAT IS IT?
I HAVE TO GET THIS GIRL OUT OF ME. I HAVE TO BE ALONE INSIDE MY SKIN, OR I'LL GO COMPLETELY CRAZY.
NOTHING.
IT'S NOTHING.
I THINK YOU NEED TO LIE DOWN. JUST UNTIL YOU FEEL BETTER.
I SHOULDN'T STAY HERE. I JUST NEED A MINUTE, AND THEN I'LL GO BACK TO THE CEMETERY.
JUST A MINUTE...
ZZZZZZZZZ

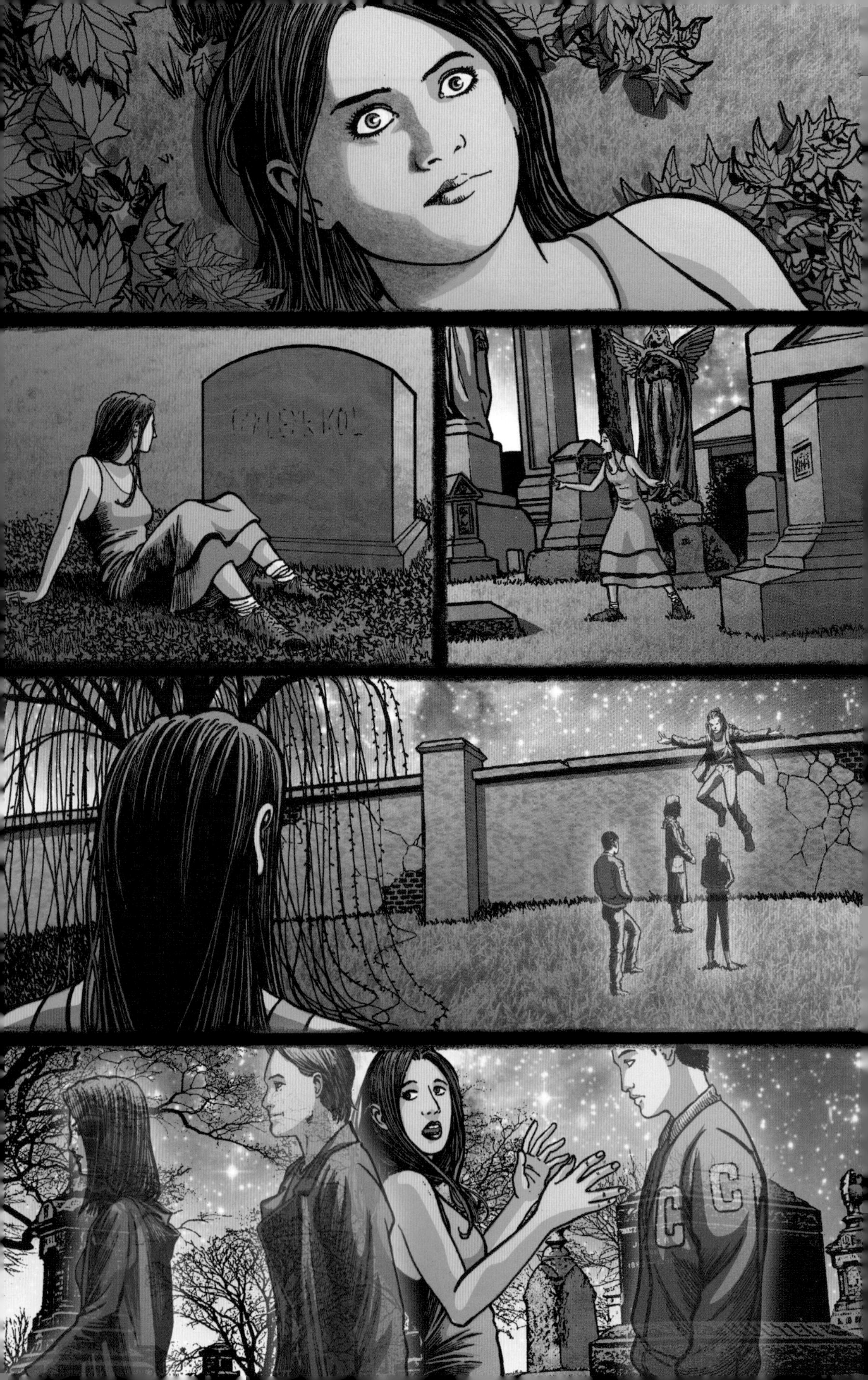

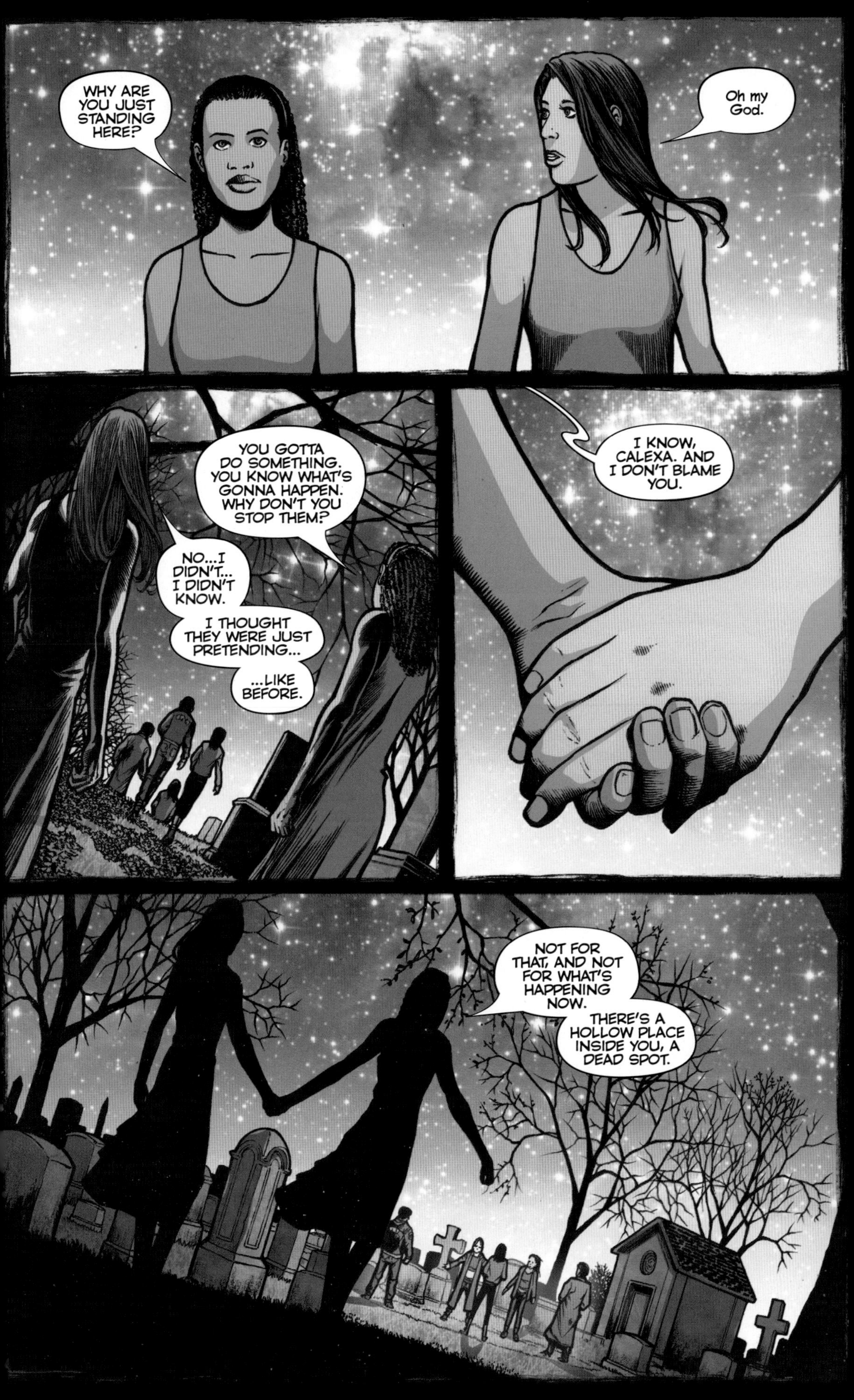
WHY ARE YOU JUST STANDING HERE?
Oh my God.
YOU GOTTA DO SOMETHING. YOU KNOW WHAT'S GONNA HAPPEN. WHY DON'T YOU STOP THEM?
NO...I DIDN'T... I DIDN'T KNOW.
I THOUGHT THEY WERE JUST PRETENDING...
...LIKE BEFORE.
I KNOW, CALEXA. AND I DON'T BLAME YOU.
NOT FOR THAT, AND NOT FOR WHAT'S HAPPENING NOW.
THERE'S A HOLLOW PLACE INSIDE YOU, A DEAD SPOT.

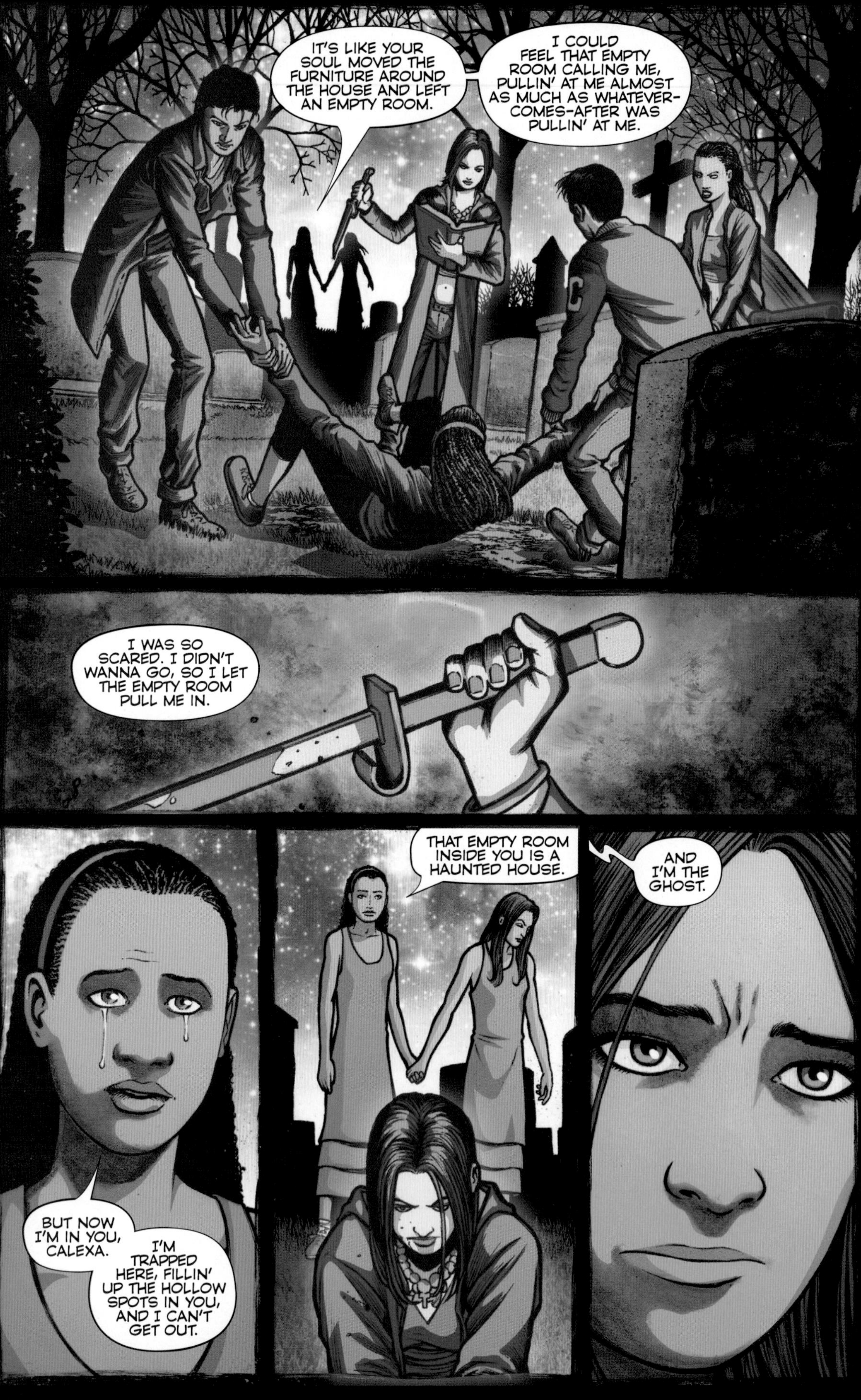
IT'S LIKE YOUR SOUL MOVED THE FURNITURE AROUND THE HOUSE AND LEFT AN EMPTY ROOM.
I COULD FEEL THAT EMPTY ROOM CALLING ME, PULLIN' AT ME ALMOST AS MUCH AS WHATEVER-COMES-AFTER WAS PULLIN' AT ME.
I WAS SO SCARED. I DIDN'T WANNA GO, SO I LET THE EMPTY ROOM PULL ME IN.
BUT NOW I'M IN YOU, CALEXA.
I'M TRAPPED HERE, FILLIN' UP THE HOLLOW SPOTS IN YOU, AND I CAN'T GET OUT.
THAT EMPTY ROOM INSIDE YOU IS A HAUNTED HOUSE.
AND I'M THE GHOST.

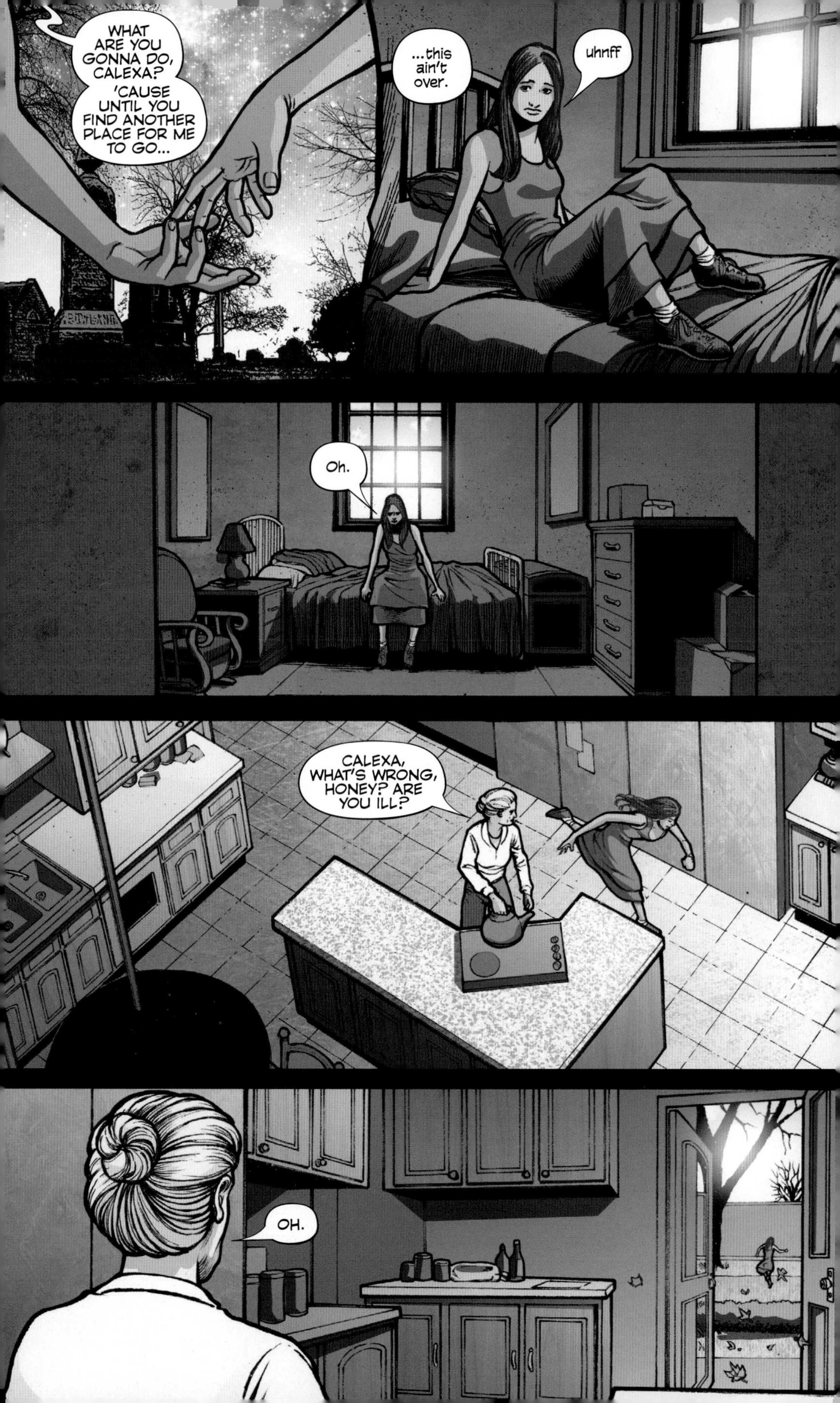
WHAT ARE YOU GONNA DO, CALEXA?
'CAUSE UNTIL YOU FIND ANOTHER PLACE FOR ME TO GO...
...this ain't over.
uhnff
Oh.
CALEXA, WHAT'S WRONG, HONEY? ARE YOU ILL?
OH.

TRUTEL

28

Maria
47 Missed Calls
93 Text Messages

Clear Alerts

Close

Settings

OmniFocus

Maps

Safari

Instacast

Gmail

I SHOULD CALL
HER MOTHER. CALL
SOMEONE.

ZACH

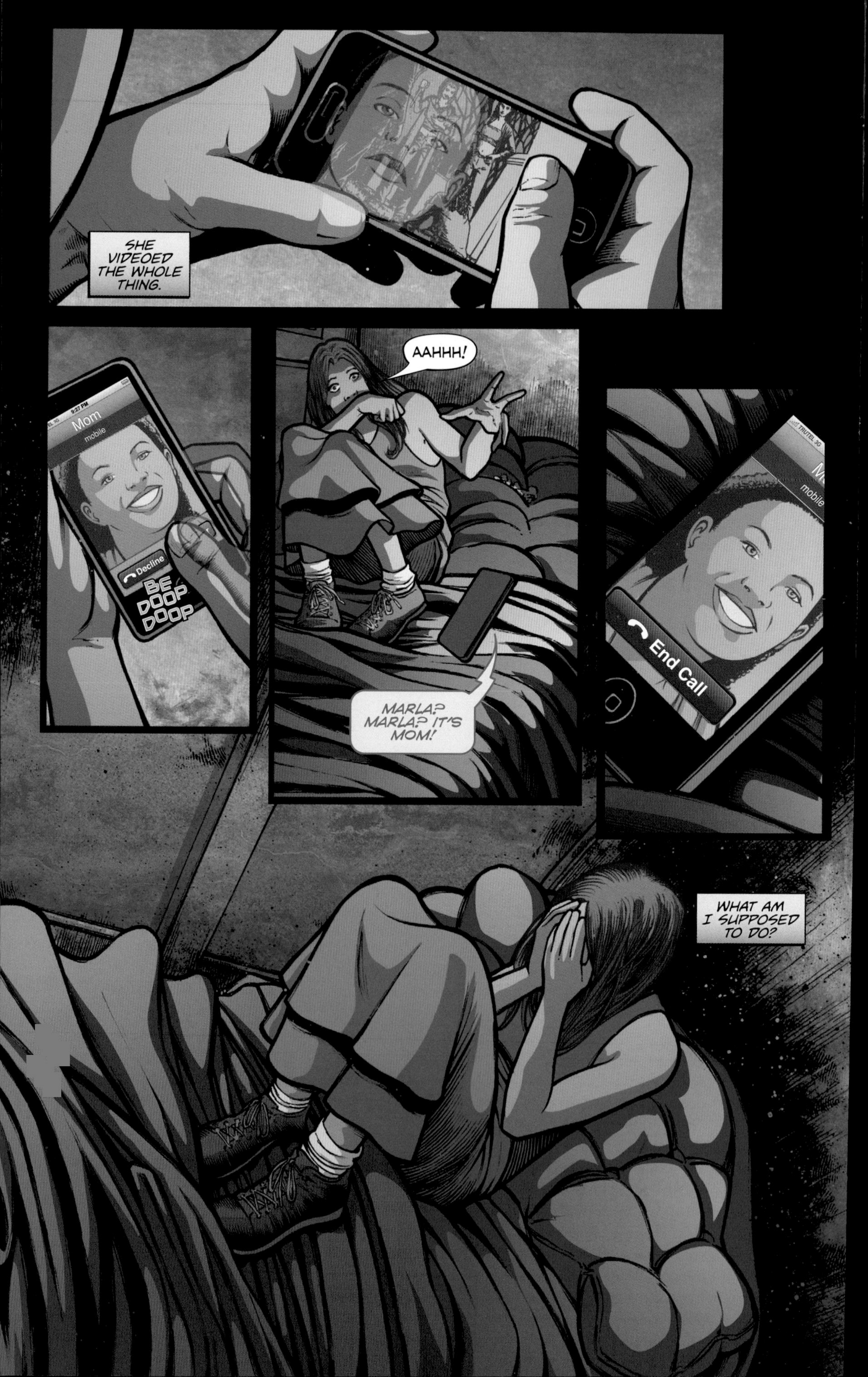
SHE VIDEOED THE WHOLE THING.
9:27 PM
Mom
mobile
Decline
BE DOOP DOOP
AAHHH!
MARLA? MARLA? IT'S MOM!
TRUTEL 3G
mobile
End Call
WHAT AM I SUPPOSED TO DO?

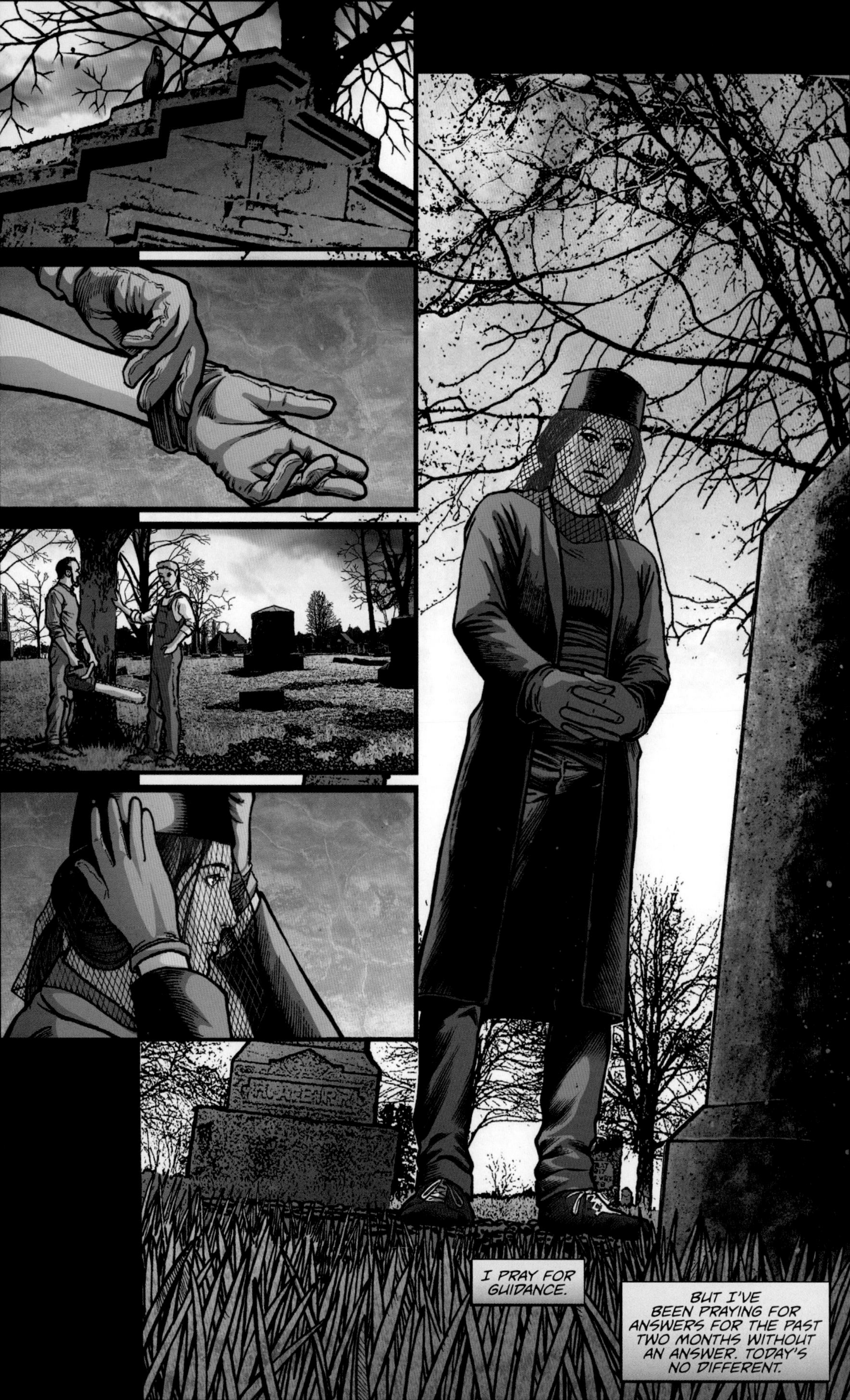
I PRAY FOR GUIDANCE.
BUT I'VE BEEN PRAYING FOR ANSWERS FOR THE PAST TWO MONTHS WITHOUT AN ANSWER. TODAY'S NO DIFFERENT.

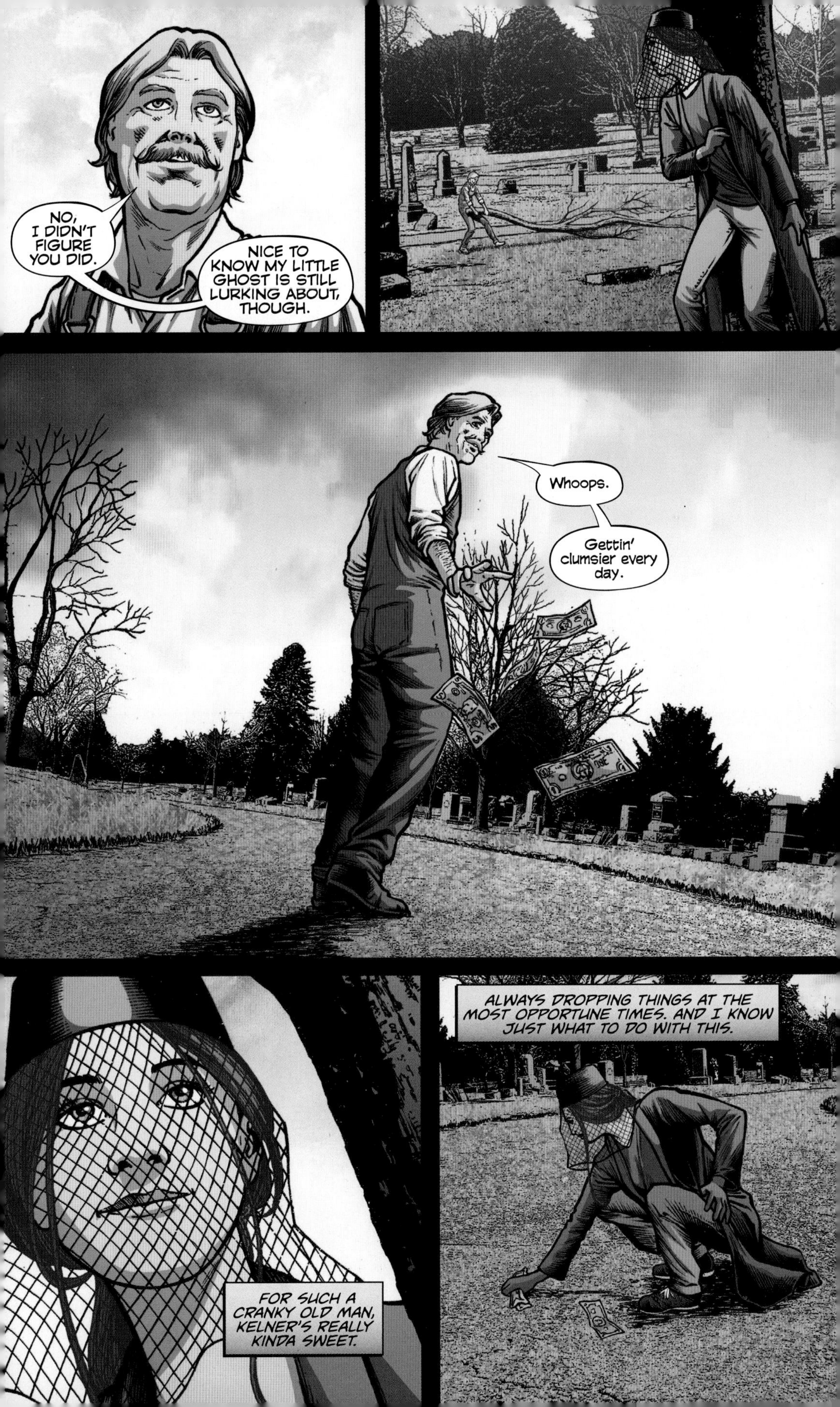
NO, I DIDN'T FIGURE YOU DID.
NICE TO KNOW MY LITTLE GHOST IS STILL LURKING ABOUT, THOUGH.
Whoops.
Gettin' clumsier every day.
FOR SUCH A CRANKY OLD MAN, KELNER'S REALLY KINDA SWEET.
ALWAYS DROPPING THINGS AT THE MOST OPPORTUNE TIMES. AND I KNOW JUST WHAT TO DO WITH THIS.

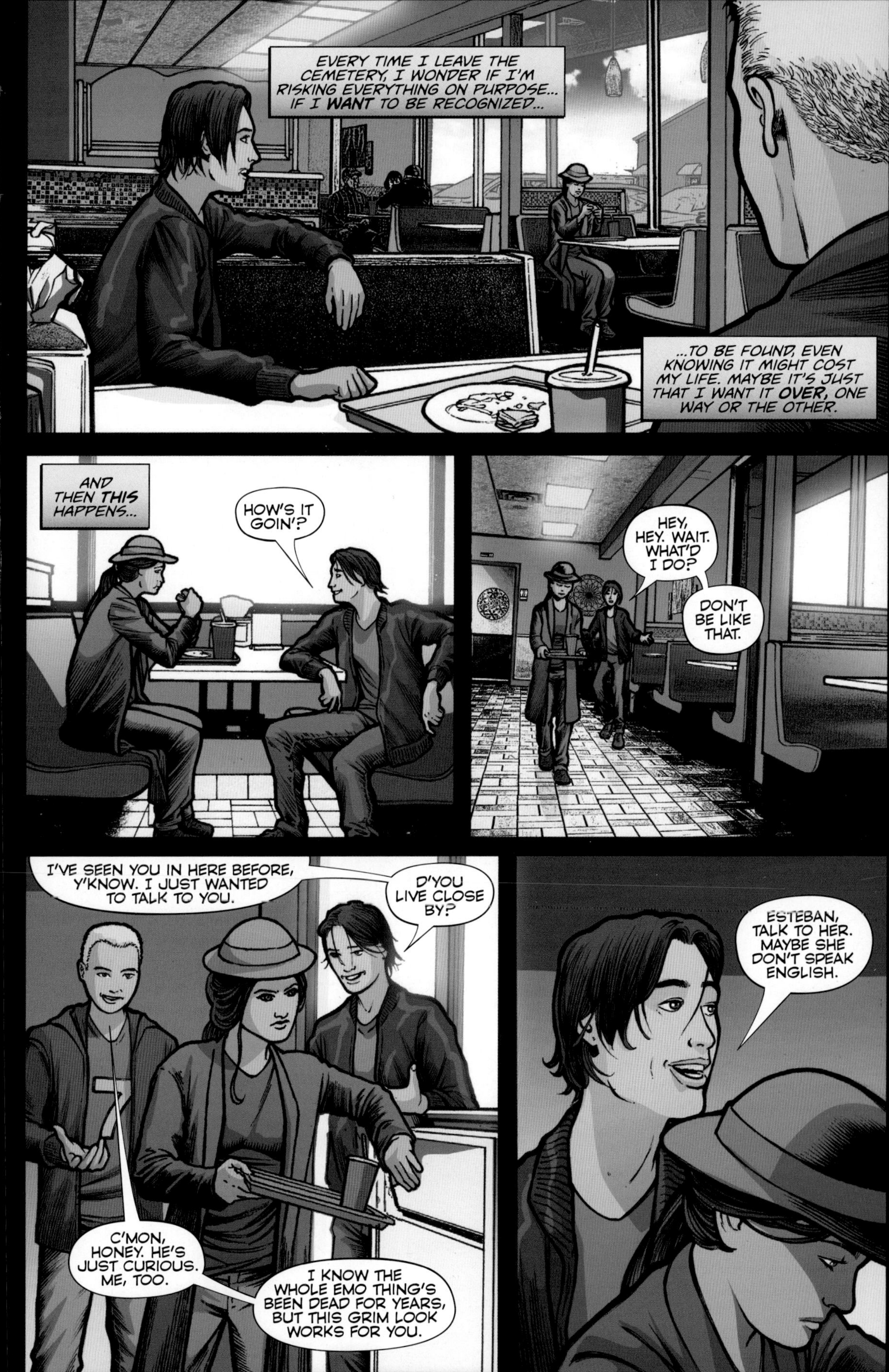
EVERY TIME I LEAVE THE CEMETERY, I WONDER IF I'M RISKING EVERYTHING ON PURPOSE... IF I WANT TO BE RECOGNIZED...
...TO BE FOUND, EVEN KNOWING IT MIGHT COST MY LIFE. MAYBE IT'S JUST THAT I WANT IT OVER, ONE WAY OR THE OTHER.
AND THEN THIS HAPPENS...
HOW'S IT GOIN'?
HEY, HEY. WAIT. WHAT'D I DO?
DON'T BE LIKE THAT.
I'VE SEEN YOU IN HERE BEFORE, Y'KNOW. I JUST WANTED TO TALK TO YOU.
D'YOU LIVE CLOSE BY?
C'MON, HONEY. HE'S JUST CURIOUS. ME, TOO.
I KNOW THE WHOLE EMO THING'S BEEN DEAD FOR YEARS, BUT THIS GRIM LOOK WORKS FOR YOU.
ESTEBAN, TALK TO HER. MAYBE SHE DON'T SPEAK ENGLISH.

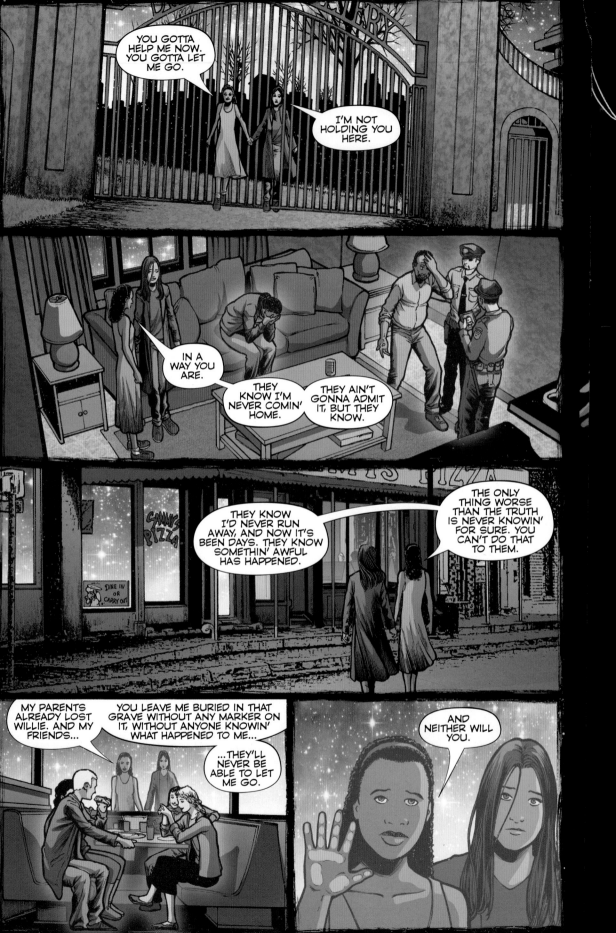

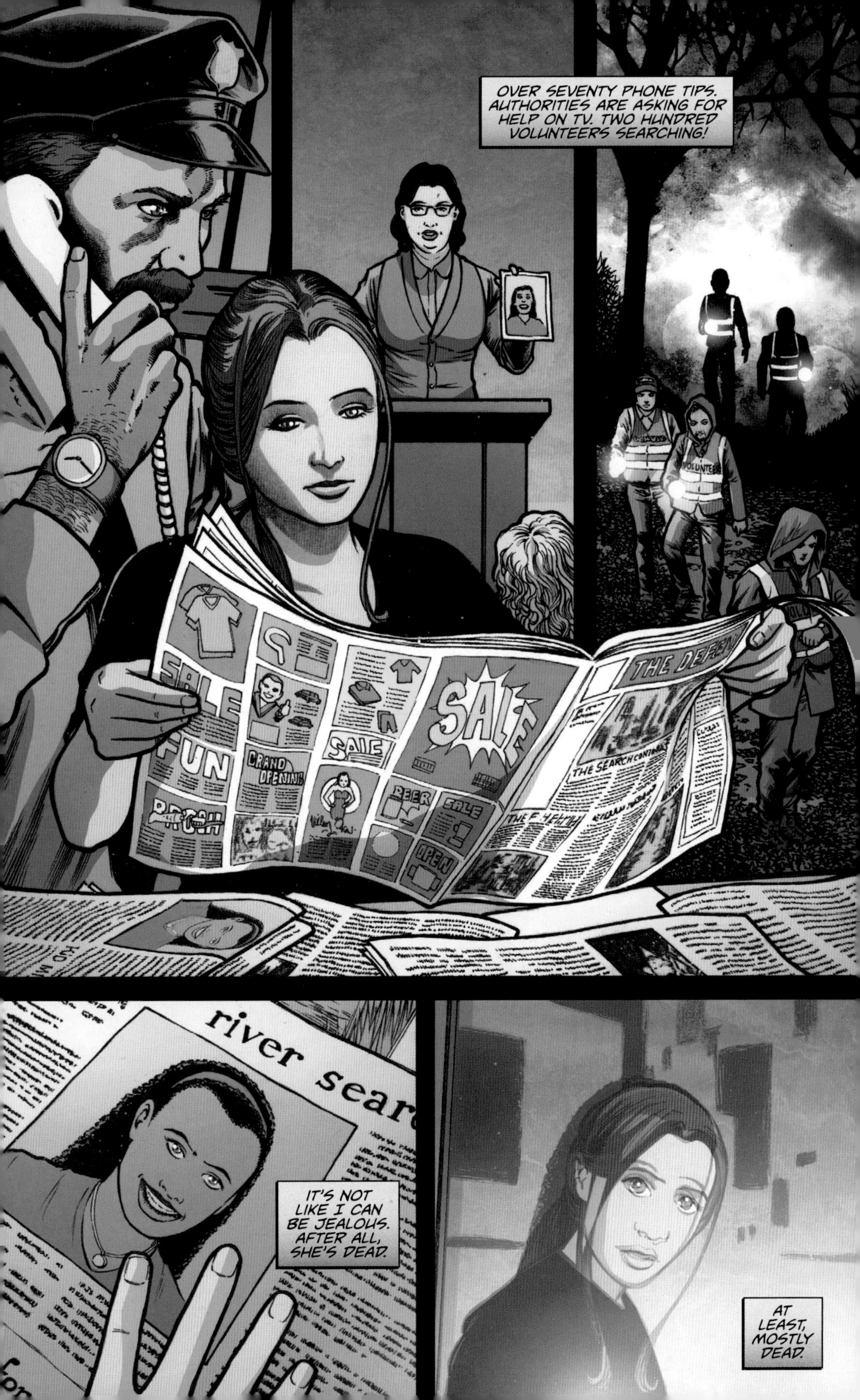
OVER SEVENTY PHONE TIPS. AUTHORITIES ARE ASKING FOR HELP ON TV. TWO HUNDRED VOLUNTEERS SEARCHING!
SALE
FUN
GRAND OPENING
SALE
BEER
SALE
OPEN
THE SEARCH CONTINUES
river sear
IT'S NOT LIKE I CAN BE JEALOUS. AFTER ALL, SHE'S DEAD.
AT LEAST, MOSTLY DEAD.

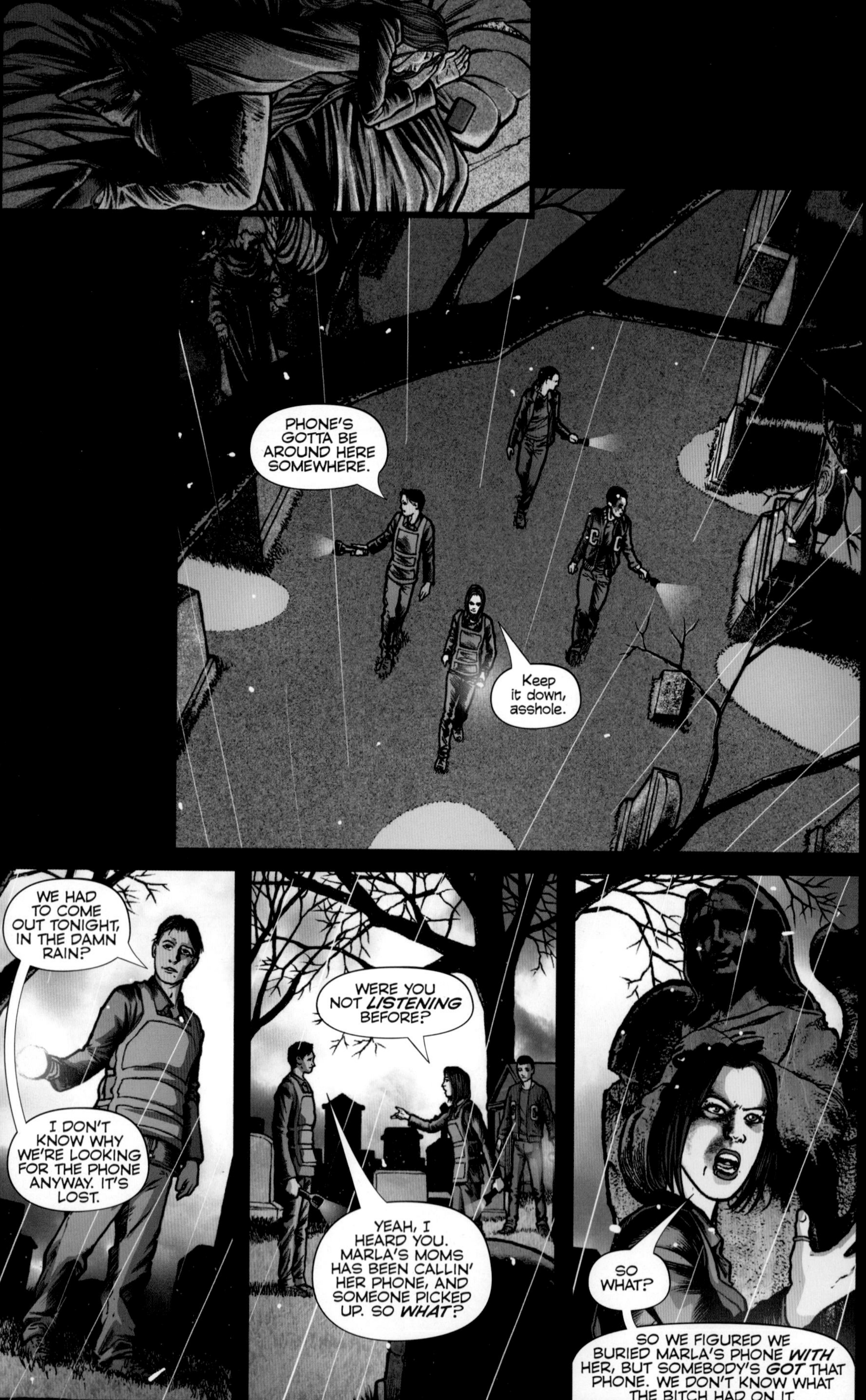
PHONE'S GOTTA BE AROUND HERE SOMEWHERE.
Keep it down, asshole.
WE HAD TO COME OUT TONIGHT, IN THE DAMN RAIN?
I DON'T KNOW WHY WE'RE LOOKING FOR THE PHONE ANYWAY. IT'S LOST.
WERE YOU NOT *LISTENING* BEFORE?
YEAH, I HEARD YOU. MARLA'S MOMS HAS BEEN CALLIN' HER PHONE, AND SOMEONE PICKED UP. SO *WHAT*?
SO WHAT?
SO WE FIGURED WE BURIED MARLA'S PHONE *WITH* HER, BUT SOMEBODY'S *GOT* THAT PHONE. WE DON'T KNOW WHAT THE BITCH HAD ON IT.

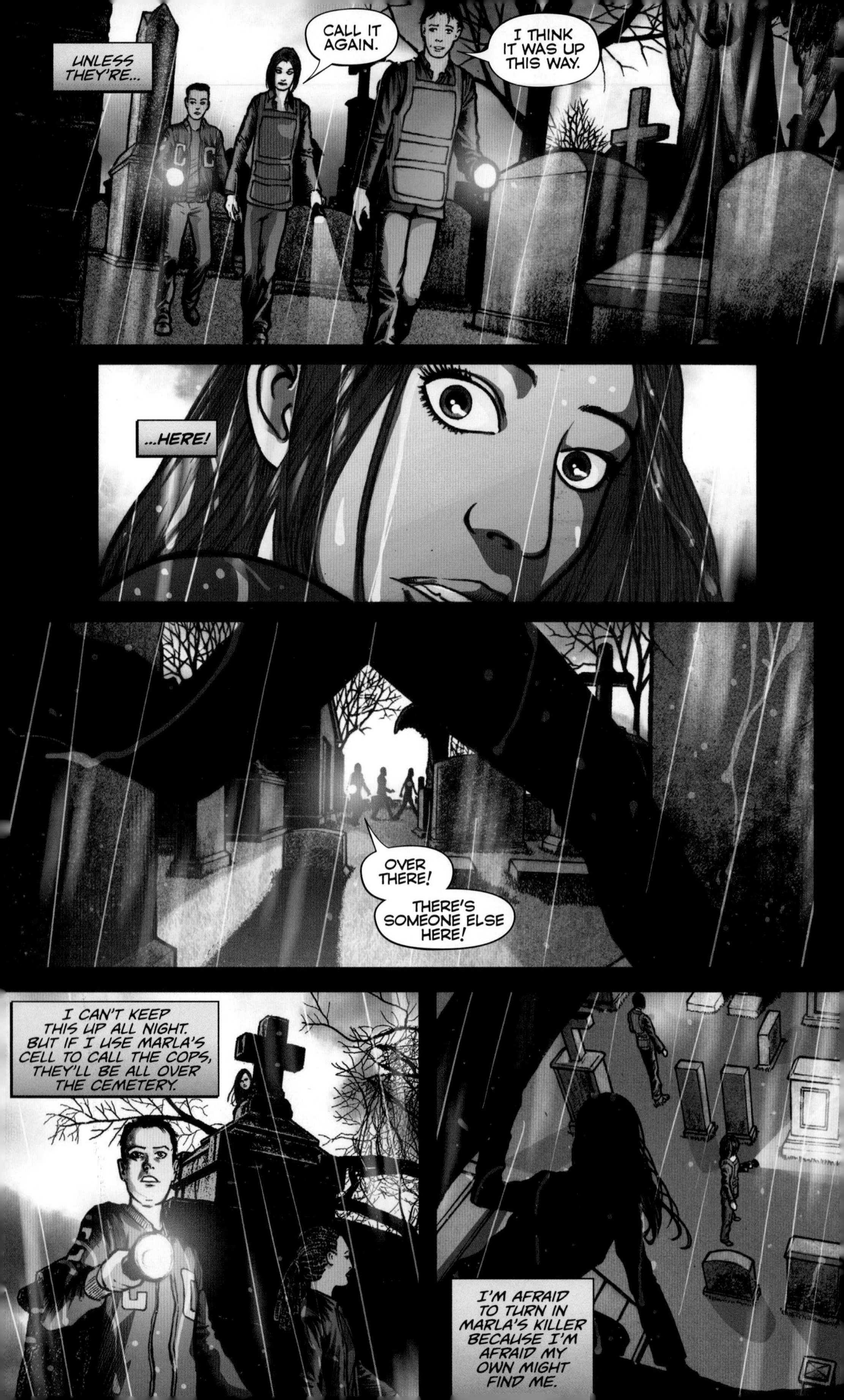
UNLESS THEY'RE...
CALL IT AGAIN.
I THINK IT WAS UP THIS WAY.
...HERE!
OVER THERE!
THERE'S SOMEONE ELSE HERE!
I CAN'T KEEP THIS UP ALL NIGHT. BUT IF I USE MARLA'S CELL TO CALL THE COPS, THEY'LL BE ALL OVER THE CEMETERY.
I'M AFRAID TO TURN IN MARLA'S KILLER BECAUSE I'M AFRAID MY OWN MIGHT FIND ME.

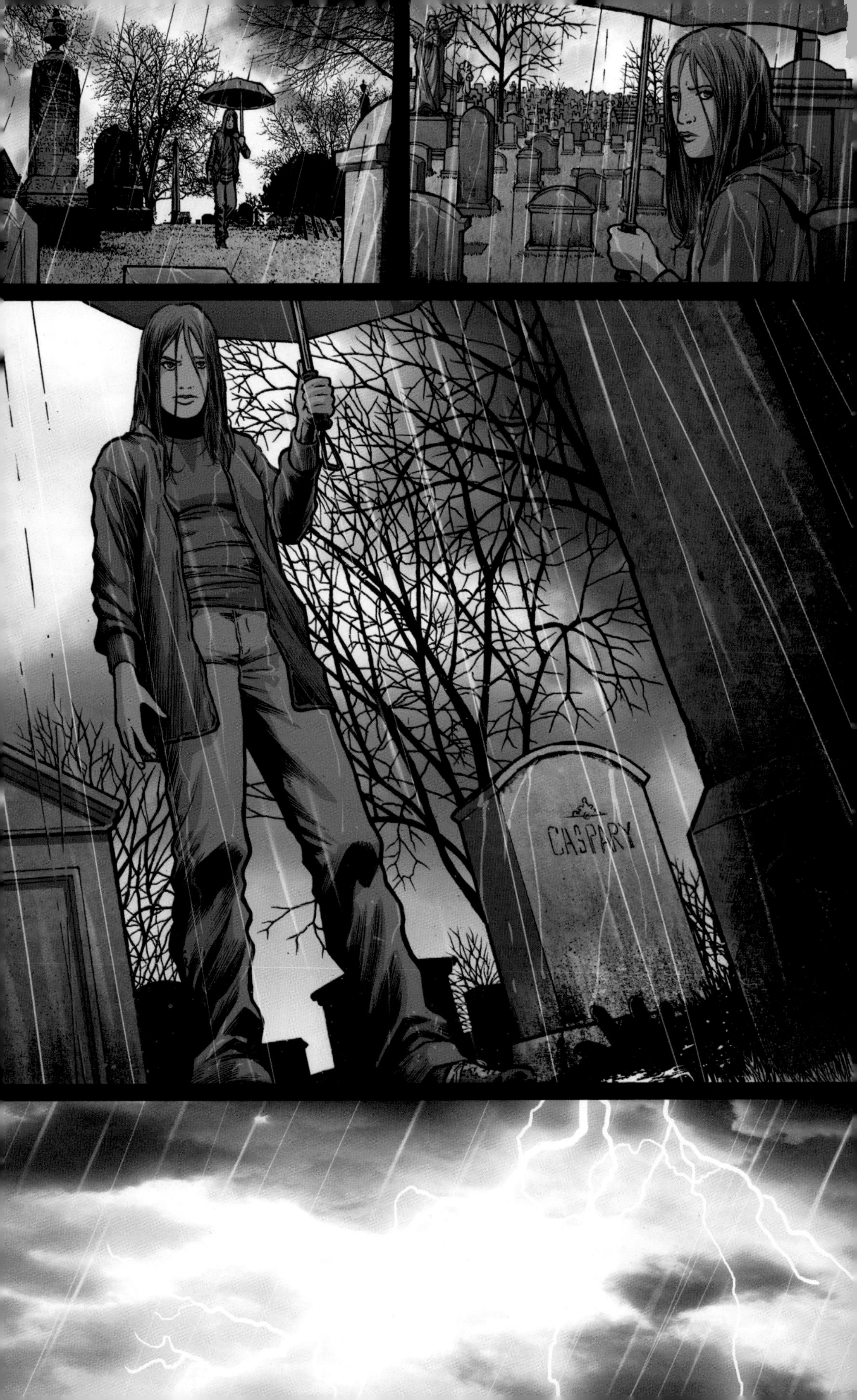
CASPARY

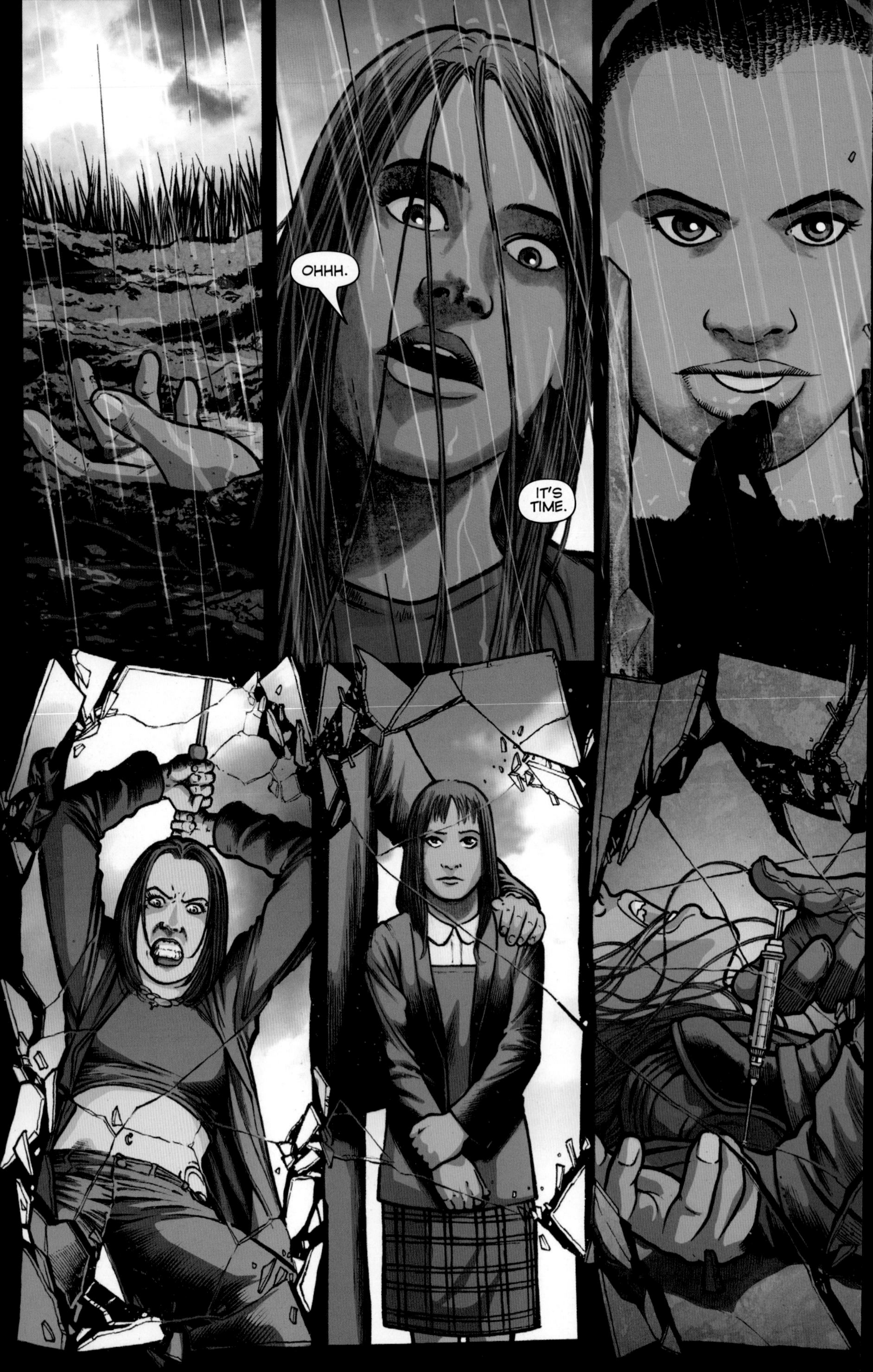
OHHH.
IT'S TIME.

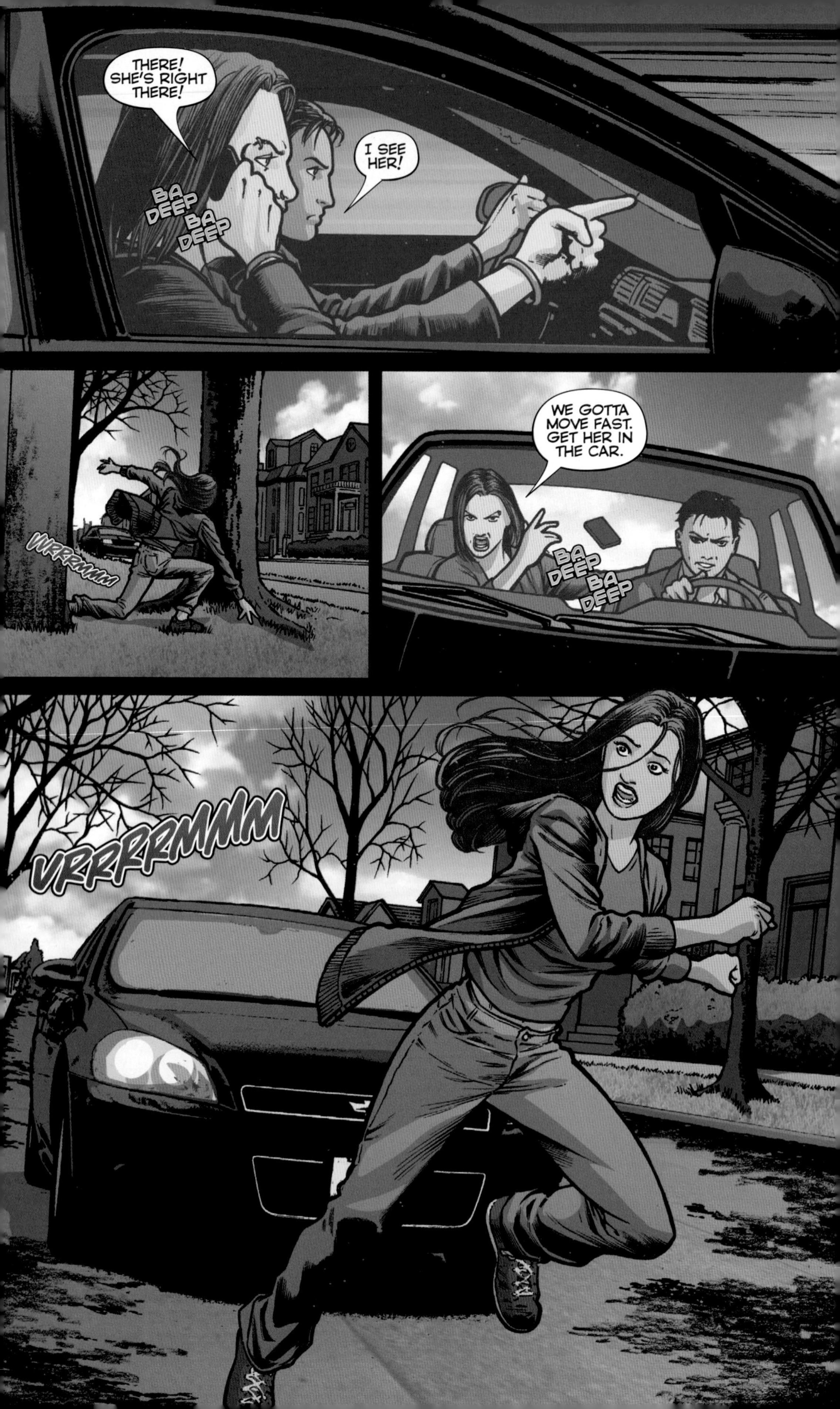
THERE! SHE'S RIGHT THERE!
BA DEEP BA DEEP
I SEE HER!
VRRRMMM
WE GOTTA MOVE FAST. GET HER IN THE CAR.
BA DEEP BA DEEP
VRRRRMMMM

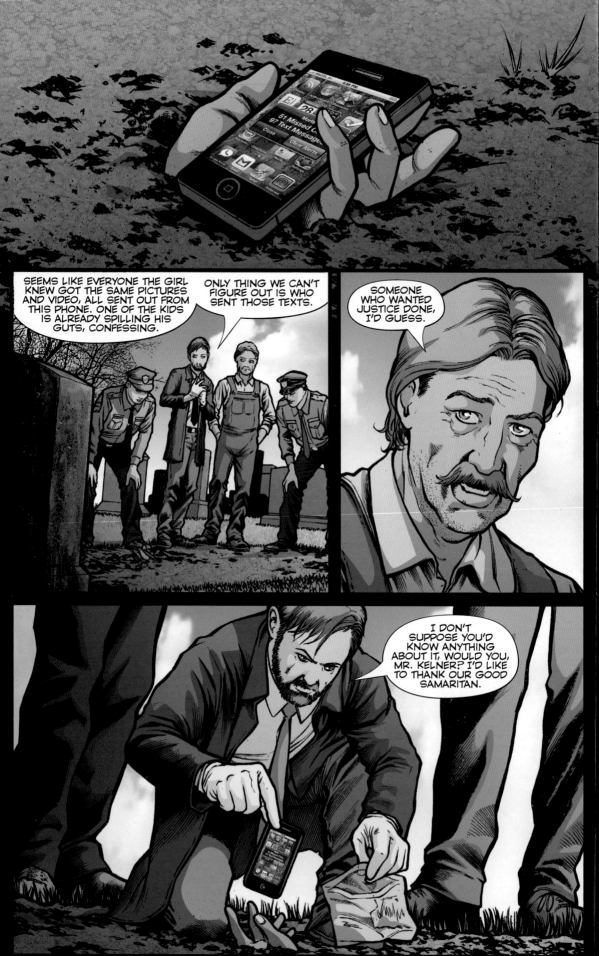

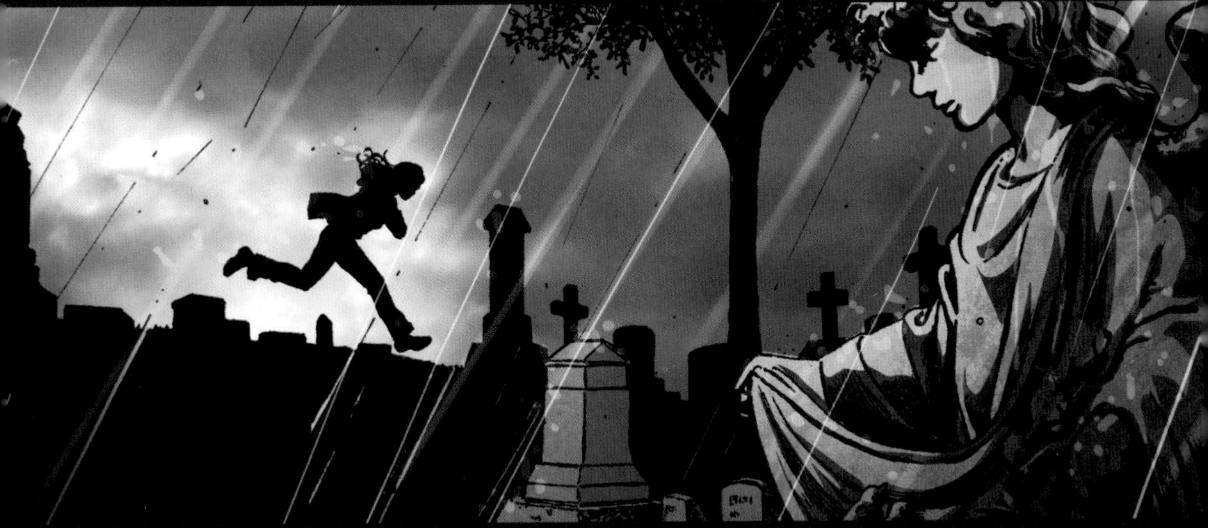

Read on for a script excerpt from
the next original graphic novel by
Charlaine Harris and Christopher Golden

Cemetery Girl

BOOK TWO: INHERITANCE

Coming soon from Jo Fletcher Books

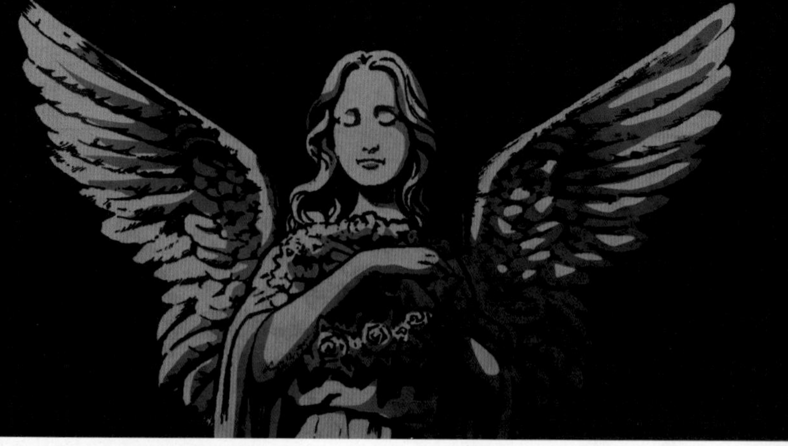

PAGE FOUR:

Panel one: Later. A shot of Lucinda's house from outside, a different angle than before and closer up. Starry sky above. The windows are all dark.

Panel two: In the bedroom she slept in at some point in book one, Calexa is asleep. The room has been made much more homey since then, with a plant and nicer bedding. She looks feverish, having kicked the covers partway off.

1/CALEXA/CAP: *I don't see Marla Vasquez in my dreams anymore. Truth is, I don't usually have dreams . . .*

Panel three: A dream/flashback. Let's do something with these panels to make clear they're not the real world. In this panel, Calexa is being injected with the serum we've hinted at, looking up in shock, realizing what has been done to her.

2/CALEXA/CAP: *For me, it's all nightmares.*

Panel four: Still in dream/flashback, she is punching someone who we see only in dream-silhouette—please try to make the person as difficult to pinpoint as possible, so it's not even clear if it's a male or female. They're in a lab, though we don't want to show what kind of lab.

3/CALEXA/CAP: *Mostly about the night I died.*

Panel five: Dream/flashback. Calexa being punched in the gut (let's see the fist but not its owner).

4/CALEXA/CAP: *If I could just see his face . . . But in my dream he's always in darkness . . .*

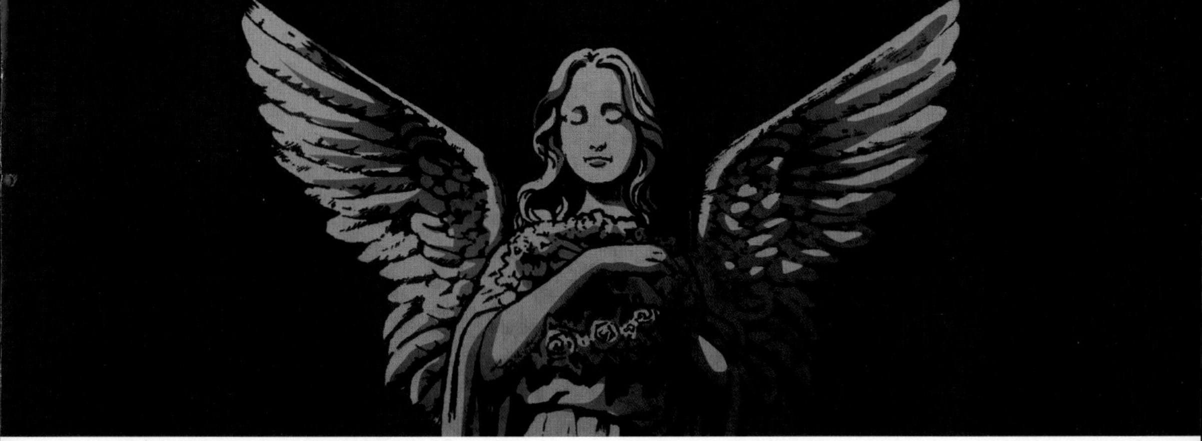

PAGE FIVE:

Panel one: Dream/flashback. Calexa being slapped hard.

1/CALEXA/CAP: *. . . always striking from the shadows.*

Panel two: Dream/flashback. Calexa crashing against a counter where there are racks of ampoules of some kind of drug. She's down on one knee, looking drugged out, turning back up toward her attacker (toward us, really).

2/CALEXA: *Why are . . . ? Why would you . . . ?*

Panel three: Dream/flashback. Calexa in a car trunk, looking dead, in the rain. (Another angle on something from book one.)

Panel four: Dream/flashback. Calexa tumbling down the slope in the rain (from book one).

3/CALEXA/CAP: *And then the dream always changes.*

Panel five: Dream/flashback. Calexa standing in the middle of the cemetery in the rain, looking around fearfully, hearing voices.

4/CALEXA/CAP: *It isn't about me anymore. It's about them.*

5/VOICE #1: *. . . Calexa . . . Help us, Calexa . . .*

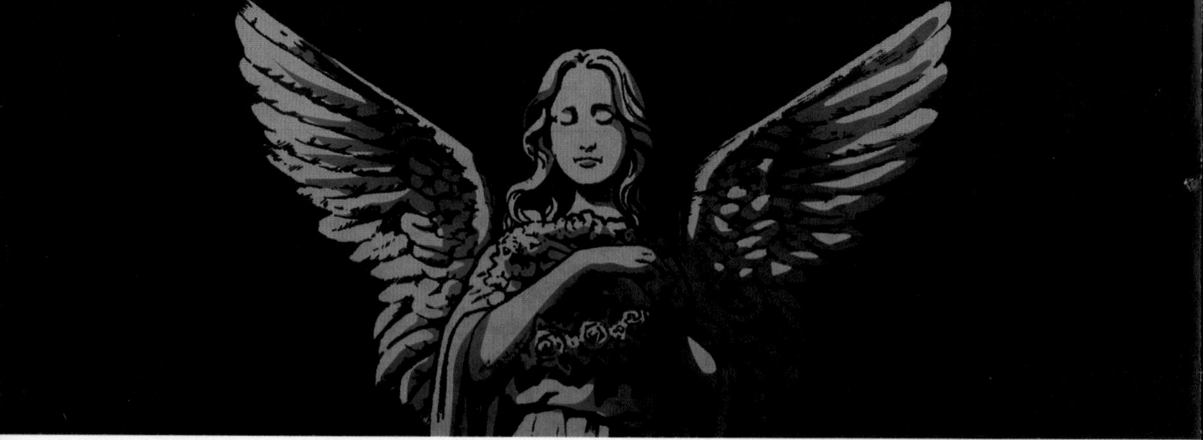

PAGE SIX:

Panel one: Dream/flashback. SPLASH!!! Similar to last panel on previous page, but now Calexa is surrounded by the ghosts of the dead rising from their graves. They've all got their hands up, reaching toward her, pleading, and she looks terrified.

> **1/CALEXA/CAP:** *All the people like Marla, whose spirits have never really been laid to rest . . . whose ghosts are uneasy because the true stories of their deaths have yet to be told.*
>
> **2/VOICE #2:** *. . . Help us, Calexa . . .*
>
> **3/VOICE #3:** *. . . Like you helped Marla . . .*
>
> **4/VOICE #1:** *. . . Help us rest . . .*

PAGE SEVEN:

Panel one: Calexa starts awake, wide-eyed and fearful. She's damp with fever, and the sheets are in total disarray.

> **1/CALEXA:** *ungghh*

Panel two: Lying back down, on her side now but with her eyes open, she stares at nothing, looking like her heart is still beating fast from the dream/nightmare.

> **2/CALEXA/CAP:** *I don't know if the ghosts in my dreams are real, but it doesn't matter.*

Panel three: She has climbed out of bed and is walking across the room toward the window, which is partway open, looking a bit like a ghost herself.

> **3/CALEXA/CAP:** *How am I supposed to help them . . .*

Panel four: She has leaned her forehead against the glass, and—somehow, Don, I'm sure you'll make this angle work—she is looking out at the cemetery across the street (and the wall, of course).

> **4/CALEXA (spoken, small letters to indicate whisper):** *. . . when I can't even help myself?*

Panel five: Calexa turns at a sound off panel. She's frowning and has hunched down a bit, almost like an animal sensing danger.

> **5/SFX (coming from off panel):** *Thumppp!*